START YOUR DREAM BUSINESS

Sarah Wade & Carole Ann Rice

START YOUR DREAM BUSINESS

SECRETS OF SUCCESSFUL AND HAPPY ENTREPRENEURS

Published in 2013 by
Marshall Cavendish Business
An imprint of Marshall Cavendish International
1 New Industrial Road, Singapore 536196

Other Marshall Cavendish Offices
Marshall Cavendish Corporation. 99 White Plains Road, Tarrytown NY 10591-9001, USA • Marshall
Cavendish International (Thailand) Co Ltd. 253 Asoke, 12th Flr, Sukhumvit 21 Road, Klongtoey Nua,
Wattana, Bangkok 10110, Thailand • Marshall Cavendish (Malaysia) Sdn Bhd, Times Subang, Lot 46,
Subang Hi-Tech Industrial Park, Batu Tiga, 40000 Shah Alam, Selangor Darul Ehsan, Malaysia

Marshall Cavendish is a trademark of Times Publishing Limited

National Library Board, Singapore Cataloguing-in-Publication Data:
Wade, Sarah.
Start your dream business : secrets of successful and happy entrepreneurs
/ Sarah Wade & Carole Ann Rice. – Singapore : Marshall Cavendish Business, 2013.
p. cm.
ISBN : 978-981-4408-13-4 (pbk.)
1. New business enterprises – Planning.   2. Small business – Management.
3. Entrepreneurship.   I. Rice, Carole Ann.   II. Title.
HD62.5
658.11 – dc23   OCN823269134

Cover art by Cover Kitchen
Printed and bound in the United Kingdom by TJ International Ltd

CONTENTS

INTRODUCTION

CAN YOU EARN good money doing something you love? And can you do it by working for yourself?

This book is for anyone who has ever had the idea of setting up their own 'dream business' but has yet to do so for a number of reasons.

It might be not wanting to give up the security of a regular salary and a pension. Or it might be the lack of know-how or being unsure of what business to start. Or it might simply be the fear of failure – the main reason people cite for not setting up on their own.

This is also a book for anyone who feels unfulfilled at work, who feels their creativity is not utilised, not appreciated, not required. It's for anyone who no longer wants a boss, or to have to ask permission for time off.

I wanted to know if there is an alternative, if something else is possible. Can you be your own boss, and succeed?

The book features interviews I have conducted with 16 entrepreneurs from around the world, each of whom has changed direction, started their own business and made a real success of it. Interestingly, for each of them, 'success' has a different meaning. And this is because they are amazingly different individuals, drawn from all walks of life.

Talking to these men and women has been fascinating. I have come to admire every one of them for their skills, their drive, and, above all, their tenacity and determination to make things happen. I very much hope you will be as inspired by them as I have been. I asked them to share their experience and demonstrate to others that it can be done.

What they have taught me is that a major part of being a successful entrepreneur is a mindset rather than a set of skills or capabilities. With the right approach, you *can* become your own boss and create something from nothing.

Each entrepreneur I interviewed was driven by a passion to solve a problem, make something amazing, or improve other people's lives – I was surprised to discover in each case it was never just about the money. As the cliché goes, they do what they love, and the money has followed.

But it's not just about having a dream and a mindset. There are practical lessons to be learned, and to that end, my co-author Carole Ann provides a wealth of good business advice at the end of each chapter.

Sarah Wade

BEING MADE REDUNDANT from the *Birmingham Post* as fashion and lifestyle editor was the best career move I didn't actually choose to make. OK, I had about three hours of heated indignation, but then I started to think about my options.

As a journalist I had enjoyed some awesome assignments – morning coffee with Terence Stamp at Fortnum and Mason, lunch with the Duchess of York, afternoon tea in a broom cupboard with Stephen Fry. I was privileged to interview such glittering names as Paloma Picasso and Lord Lichfield, and get sent on international assignments from Moscow to New York.

Yet all of it pales in comparison with the sheer thrill of retraining to be a life coach and the joy of being my own boss and having my own business.

True, I don't have sick leave, paid holidays or a big group of colleagues to conspire and socialise with. But I choose my hours, work with incredible people who have also turned my life around, make more money than in any previous 'paid' employment and get 100 percent job satisfaction.

I've been at home to see my children grow and I've never missed a nativity play. I have a great work-life balance, and most precious of all, I have complete autonomy.

The satisfaction of seeing my business grow, discovering new skills (such as public speaking and social media), making my own money and discovering new ways to increase my profits is immense.

Business owners are different. They have that five-mile stare, that look of not being quite with you as they ponder their towering to-do lists whilst keeping their eyes firmly fixed on their vision and beyond.

They look a little dark around the eyes from late nights, not switching off and getting up early in the eternal pursuit of 'catching up.'

They are optimistic types interested in new ideas. Dreaming big is what they do best. Tired but happy they passionately put in the hours to service clients' needs, meet orders or design new offers for their businesses, and they always love to hear how others in business have 'made it.'

Oh, and they know the power of good shoes. After all, when you've put in all that hard work you have to have the occasional treat.

Why not join us? Yes, it's scary, there are risks aplenty and few guarantees. But it is a life well lived and the rewards are manifold.

Of course the market is flooded – but trust me, there is always limitless room for success.

See you at the top.

Good luck!

Carole Ann Rice

CHAPTER 1

Starting out:
From baby steps to giant leaps

66 You see, Dorothy, you had the power within you all along. **99**

Glinda the Good Witch
The Wizard of Oz

66 *'Follow your passion' – I used to read things like that and think they were really corny. But you can't tell me I'm not heading in the right direction. I was on the front page of the local paper, and my 'muse' milliner contacted me to say she's so inspired by what I'm doing!* 99

Christie Stokes

U NLIKE THE other entrepreneurs in this book, who are well-established in their businesses, Christie is just starting out. But her story illustrates the dilemmas for anyone contemplating starting their own business. This is a book about entrepreneurs and why they are successful. I wanted to include Christie because she captures many of the realities and practicalities of the first steps of the process. Her life would be considerably easier if she had just stayed in her day job. It would also be a lot less rewarding and fun.

DREAM BUSINESS OWNER

Christie Stokes
Founder,
Christie Millinery Designs,
Gold Coast, Australia

JOURNEY

Physiotherapist ➡ Milliner

All the contributors to this book changed direction to do something different. They often created something from nothing or were driven to solve a problem. Likewise Christie is torn between a sensible job with its lure of a regular salary and a new-found passion that brings unmitigated joy whenever she does it. She is cramming millinery around her day job, but just doesn't feel confident enough to make the leap and do it full-time. She is a work in progress. But sometimes you get to meet people and you just sense from their drive, mindset and commitment that they are going to be successful. Indeed, Christie has already achieved much success in her short business career.

In a later story, we find out that Penny wanted to train as a physiotherapist, failed to get onto the course and therefore turned to the world of business. In this story, our heroine Christie *did* train as a physiotherapist – and became a good one. But she had only just turned 16 when she embarked on it and, with hindsight, suspects she was too young to understand what she was getting herself into.

"I suppose I took the safe route. I was artistic but I enjoyed science. At the back of my head I knew if I did science I would get a job. And I wanted a solid job, so I didn't pursue arts.

"When I graduated from physiotherapy, it was extremely taxing and stressful. When I got into the workplace I thought, 'Oh my god, I spent the last five and a half years of my life for this?' It was a big shock. But I thought, 'I have to give this a chance, I've spent so long working at it.' But I'd always been drawn to something more. I wish someone had sat me down and asked me, 'Why are you doing this?' I don't even look the part. I'm not your typical physio with an athletic, sporty build. I always get mistaken for the receptionist because I'm fairly petite and dress quite nicely.

"As a physio, there's the mental stress of diagnosing people, looking at the scans. There's the emotional stress of dealing with people in pain. You're trying to make them feel better. You feel sorry for them. Often they're upset. And physically it's stressful because you're massaging and prodding all day long. There aren't many jobs that involve all three of those stresses. And a lot of people burn out."

Christie travelled with her fiancé to Canada, where she continued working as a physiotherapist to fund her travels.

"While in Canada I found myself in a hat shop and lost myself in there for an hour. I couldn't even describe it. It was the weirdest sensation ever. At university, I used to make fascinators for the university races. I'd often thought of doing it on the side, but now I suddenly found myself engrossed in studying the hats! Then I came home for a wedding and visited the Gallery of Modern Art in Brisbane for a hat exhibition with my sister – and I had the exact same feeling. I just felt, 'I've got to do this, it's all-consuming – yet I've never really done it before!'"

I can't do this

"I was devastated by the prospect of returning to Australia from Canada and settling down, getting married, having kids and being a physio for the rest of my life. I just thought, 'I can't do this.'"

Christie started looking into millinery and found a course in Melbourne.

"We were travelling, we were on the move, so packing up and relocating to a new city wasn't a big deal. Melbourne is one of the hubs of millinery in the world and I found a course there that would allow me to fund myself through physio four days a week.

My fiancé had already got a job at the other end of Australia – and that was a big deal. But I Skyped the college from Canada and they said that they could fit me in. So that was it. We got back and, having been together for three years, went to opposite ends of Australia. It was definitely challenging. Luckily I completely lost myself in millinery. And then, in the end, my fiancé came to live in Melbourne.

"One day I came home from a millinery course and sat down. My fiancé looked at me and said, 'Are you OK?' Instead of answering, I put a question to him. 'Do you actually enjoy going to work?' He said, 'Yeah.' He's a carpenter and he loves it. Then I asked him, 'Do you get home and think, wow, that was just awesome?' And he said, 'Yeah.' I said, 'I've just had that for the first time ever today.'"

Realisation

"I had been thinking, 'Maybe I'll do millinery part-time as a hobby.' But that was the turning point. It's what life's about. We spend most our lives working. So if I don't have this kind of passion and it's not giving me the joy that I need in the greater part of my life, it's not for me." So Christie set about starting her own company.

"As a physio I've always worked for other people. People used to ask me if I wanted to open my own physio business. 'Do you have that passion?' And my answer was always, 'No!' But with this, it's completely effortless. When I wake up in the morning, it's all I think about. Pouring myself into it is all I want to do. It gives me so much joy and energy.

"Of course, I'm flipping my whole career on its head. My background is science and very structured. I've never been a fashionista. But now I need to learn about fashion. I need to learn about working for myself. I also need to learn about the web – I've never been hugely internet-savvy. And then there's PR. I'm so unbelievably out of my depth!"

Making a start

"I've done a lot of research into the industry, and I've spent hours looking at small-business blogs. When I was in Melbourne it gave me a bit of insider knowledge of Australian millinery, but it's very much a work in progress. I'm currently doing another three years of millinery through Queensland Technical and Further Education in Brisbane. It includes some business elements, so I am going to get to learn a little bit of the fashion business relating to millinery.

"At this stage, a lot of my research is web-based. I have another friend who is making handbags and she's a couple of years ahead of where I am. She sent me some books on fashion and business. I also have amazing support from my little sister who, unlike me, is really savvy about the internet and IT.

"I haven't done a business plan yet. This is where my complete lack of experience shows. In Melbourne I found some young, funky outlets to sell my stuff but it didn't really work. Then I tried an online market stall and I created my own shop on that. I was picked as their feature of the week but I only sold one or two pieces. It's such a hard industry to crack. There are quite a lot of closed doors. Someone got in touch and offered to sell my pieces on her website for commission, but that wasn't successful either. People I was directing to the internet couldn't even find me, so my sister said, 'Let's make you a website,' and she did."

Having had the nerve to pursue her passion and now going public via a website, Christie has been encouraged by the reaction. "I'm very conscious that I've got so much to learn. But I crave professional and personal development. I launched my website a month ago and it just took off from there. And, of course, there was the Melbourne Cup!"

In 2011 Christie won the Melbourne Cup Millinery Design student award for a red-and-black polka dot hat. "It completely blew me away. Picking the paper up and seeing myself on the front page was also pretty awesome. That would never happen for a physio. And my 'muse' milliner contacted me to say she's so inspired by what I'm doing!

"I'm still working pretty much full-time as a physiotherapist because I have to at the moment, in order to fund the equipment and the things that I need to continue in millinery. It's just a hard phase. I'm even looking into grants. So I'm very much in that transition phase. Over the last year I've probably only sold about ten pieces. I'm aiming to get into bridal shops because that's a good way to regularly fund my business. Then do PR and get regular commission work."

Christie's biggest challenge

"Letting go of all that's secure, and the fear of the unknown. I have been working towards being a physiotherapist for 13 years.

It's nearly half my life. Now, I've turned my back on my profession. To let that go is very scary.

"At the moment I'm having to do all these extra shifts as a physio because my fiancé is finding it hard to find work in the recession. I'm not as confident as I might be in letting go of hours to continue growing my business. We don't have secure jobs and it's tricky to drop a profession or find financial security when times are hard. There are not a lot of jobs out there and to follow your dreams at the moment is difficult. It's an odd time to pursue a career in something that really only people with a disposable income would be able to purchase.

"However, I have no doubt I'm going to succeed. I have never been more sure about anything. It's so weird. Last night in class we were watching this millinery video and I felt my insides were just bubbling. I had this massive smile on my face. It gives me so much joy. My parents have always encouraged us to push ourselves out of our comfort zone, and a good friend of mine says, 'Leap and your net will appear.' I don't know if it's an intuitive thing, but I'm simply not afraid about the future. I'm so lucky at 29 to have found my passion in life and I can't wait for how everything's going to evolve now. Whereas with physiotherapy I was dreading the future, with millinery I'm so excited about it I just know that I can't fail."

What would Christie have done differently?

"Millinery is something I could have pursued earlier if I'd listened to my gut instinct. I wish I'd got some guidance on it before I went overseas, some mentors. But the upside of physiotherapy is

Christie's Secrets
TO DREAM BUSINESS SUCCESS

66

1 Be willing to take risks. I really want to make the most out of my life. You only have one life.

2 Bring someone 'businessy' on board. I wish I'd brought somebody in who had more knowledge rather than try to do it all by myself. I would have saved a lot of time if someone who already had that background knowledge could have pointed me in the right direction. I took on too much.

99

it's given me strong hands! You need strong hands for millinery. Moreover it pays well – millinery is so expensive I'd be really struggling if I was waitressing."

Christie's inspiration

"Jane Taylor is a great success story. She started off in the UK and did a design degree in Scotland, worked under someone to get herself set up and then branched out to run her own business. She started to get a name for herself making these really high-quality couture pieces in the races that were modern and different. And young women were wearing them. She has people working for her now. And she's one of Kate Middleton's milliners!

"It's a tiny niche industry, so it's really hard to find mentors. I've been putting feelers out everywhere and asking where do I go next? But it's good to hear success stories so that you know that you can make it, too."

Social networking

"My business would not exist without social networking. Every day I'm getting feedback from people. It's provided me with so many connections. All my material is bought online because they don't supply from shops, only warehouses all around the world. It's a very small, but global, community, and there are millinery academies now. So LinkedIn and blogs are key. For me it's been so exciting to find a global network of support. I'm getting 2000 hits a week on Facebook, compared to 100 on my web page. It's just the way of the future. Business will be 70–80 percent online in the next few years. If you don't go with it you're going to fall off."

COACHING TIPS #1
Start your dream business

You don't have to have a revolutionary, innovative or totally original idea to set up in business – just look at all the hairdressers, boutiques, cafés, gift shops and online services there are out there. It is entirely possible to go into business and create a niche for yourself in an already busy and competitive market. Ignore the phrase 'flooded market' – if we all listened to that nobody would train as a coach, dentist, mechanic, beauty therapist or travel consultant. Find your niche, define your USP (Unique Selling Proposition) and you have a good chance of standing out.

Just be sure you start to hone how you will be different – what value will you add, what 'novelty' can you bring, why would people buy from you?

Have the foggiest idea

Just as there is never a 'right' time to start a family or have another child, so it is with launching a business. Some say a recession is a great time to start a new venture while others wait for the wave of prosperity or market interest to rise before they dive in. Only you can decide this.

But first you must allow the vision to form:

- Who would be your target market?

- What do you offer that others don't?

- How will you add value?

- What will set you apart and what will you be known for?

- What will really excite you and therefore your market?

What excites you will be the fuel to sustain your vision. Your passion and energy will get you through the labour pains of starting a business and the more you believe in what you do, the more others will, too.

Bit by bit piece together your idea. Take one step at a time. Research, delve, shadow others who are making it, moonlight in similar businesses, throw yourself into your idea.

Overcoming the initial obstacles

Just as your heart skips a beat when you think of having your own business, so it is that a great boulder of dread clunks down into your stomach when the realities of such an awesome adventure start to look real.

Here are the common gremlins that arise when you take a reality check:

- The huge risk, both financial and personal

- Fear of failure (How they'll laugh!) and fear of success (What if nobody likes me when I get my Maserati?)

- No guarantees it will work

- Mortgage/debt worries

- No more wages, holiday pay, sick leave, compassionate leave, paid-for training, bonuses and packages

- Self-doubt – am I good enough? Is the idea good enough?

- How to get and keep clients/customers

- Isolation, no colleagues

- Losing face

- Horrifying, all-consuming, root-you-to-the-spot fear

But counter these issues with positive thoughts:

- No boss – hurrah, you're the boss now!

- As much holiday as you like

- The creative and intellectual challenge of crafting a business

- All your labour, sweat and tears is 100 percent for you, your vision and your bank account

- You set the rules and call the shots

- Satisfaction, dream fulfilment

- Pride

- The sky's the limit

- Wealth, fame, growth, legacy

Everyone starting a business knows that there are no guarantees. But in the contemporary economic climate the same can be said of paid employment. Change is a constant, no job is for life and there are always risks on the horizon. This is the case in both paid employment and self-employment. Remember this point.

Everyone starts out in business with high hopes and big doubts so you are not alone. It is learning to manage your fears, negative beliefs and naysayers that will be the keys to your success.

Toolbox tips

So write out your current beliefs about starting your business. Are there any undermining thoughts? For example, could you be thinking:

- "People with my upbringing can't make it in business."

- "What if I make so much money my family will envy and alienate me?"

- "I need to prove myself, but what if I fail?"

- "People will see straight through me."

- "I think I have to do a three-year business degree."

- "I can't live with ambiguity and I may not survive if it all fails."

- "Am I up to it? Am I hungry enough to succeed?"

You see how our inner pessimist can bring us to our knees before we've even drawn up a business plan.

So write out the opposite of your negative thoughts – with mantras such as:

- "I *can* do this."

- "I deserve success."

- "I am a money magnet."

- "I will survive all the storms."

- "I am capable of creating abundance."

- "Who I am is more than enough."

- "I will survive and live a life well-lived."

- "Je ne regrette rien."

Say these things enough times until you believe them.

So here is the first really important lesson, which you must learn before you do anything else. Every ingredient you need to make your business successful will come from *you*.

Your energy, drive, passion, excitement, vision, belief and will to succeed will be driven almost entirely in the early stages by you. You are 100 percent responsible for your success. You can either enable success or stand in its way.

Later in the book we will be looking at how to get support, overcome difficulties and maintain your energy. But in the meantime your business will be you and you will be your business.

- If you had nothing to prove, what would you do right now to get your business off the ground?

- If you knew ahead of the game that you would achieve success, what would you do differently now?

- What is the smallest step (research, phone call, appointment) you can make today to take you one step closer to your dream business?

- What would success look like to you? Is it working three days a week, having a holiday home, a six-figure income, a franchise empire or the same as you are earning with your previous job but more downtime? Write out what success would look like three years from now.

Every journey starts with the first step and nothing comes of nothing. No more analysis paralysis. Time for action.

CHAPTER 2

Retraining for business: *Get hungry then double it*

66 Most of the people who got into the Forbes 400 got there by having an idea and pursuing that idea as long as they could. And it created great wealth for them. They didn't really care about making the money so much as pursuing the idea. 99

David Rubenstein

"You go through life sometimes and think, 'Do I know what I really like in life or do I just consume things?'"

Chai Patel

CHAI IS tremendously successful in financial terms but what drives him is something beyond money. As a successful doctor in the NHS he felt unable to fulfil his purpose in life to help people. He left and retrained in a different capacity in the corporate world in order to realise his ambitions.

DREAM BUSINESS OWNER

Dr Chai Patel CBE
Chairman, HC-One
care-home provider, UK

JOURNEY

NHS doctor ➡
Care-home entrepreneur
and philanthropist

Born in Uganda, he left with his family during the rule of Idi Amin. After spending a few years in India, they moved to Britain, where Chai spent his teenage years on a London council estate where his parents ran a post office.

Chai worked as an NHS doctor for six years before leaving medicine to work in the city. He went on to become the founder of Court Cavendish care homes and more recently chairman of HC-One, which runs 241 care homes in Britain.

"I didn't feel the NHS was fulfilling my vocational expectations of why I went into healthcare. I also felt I was unable to change things within the NHS. The motivation was to go out, do my own thing, and create a healthcare company so at least I could have some say in organising it, running it, and delivering the care and the quality that I believe in. I wanted to make a difference, to help people."

He decided to follow the private, commercial model and deliver a service he felt he could be proud of. It wasn't about being a successful businessman. It was about direct accountability to the customer. He wanted to work to serve the patients', rather than the system's, needs.

Retraining as a banker

"If I was going to set up my own healthcare company, I needed to retrain and learn about money. And having no money to invest, I needed to make some. The City was the route to doing that."

Thus Chai embarked on his career change from doctor to banker.

"I turned up at this office in the City and thought, 'Oh my god the cleaning lady knows more than I do!' It was incredible. No one really cared that I was a research fellow from Oxford. I was just at the bottom of the food chain and I had to go and get the coffees. It was quite a big culture shock and blow to my self-esteem.

"It was a steep learning curve and I wanted to learn. I was with many people I could absorb information from. I read and studied every hour to understand markets, economics, companies and businesses, sales, management, time management and all the other disciplines. I started buying the *Harvard Business Review* because medicine works through case-studies. I voraciously read company case-studies about how they were run, what worked and didn't work. It was like doing an MBA by myself."

Four years after he left medicine, Chai commissioned a piece of research into the healthcare sector to see what the issues were. It was the cash-fuelled 80s and he could have carried on making money, but he wanted to make a difference.

"Banking didn't make me happy. It's not what motivates me. I could have had a nice, comfortable life but banking wasn't what I wanted to wake up to every morning.

"My wife was upset and fearful. Why would I give up this incredible job? What were the motives? For me, it was just an adventure – like sailing the Seven Seas, searching for distant lands, or wandering off up mountains. Except we don't do all that anymore. So for me, *this* was my adventure. This was my extreme sport – my adrenalin kick, if you like."

Court Cavendish

Chai founded his first company – a long-term care services business called Court Cavendish. He recalls the excitement of buying the first care home, working there, doing the food shopping and being involved in how care was delivered. His sense of fulfillment when writing the first staff handbook and the first mission statement – these were the things that created the culture and values of the company.

"It was immensely challenging. There was a huge risk very quickly. I took a huge drop in income and nearly went bust. For a long time I couldn't even think of myself as a businessman or an entrepreneur. I was really a medic trying to solve a problem, using a commercial model.

"*Commitment to care, comfort and consideration* – that was our strapline, and that's what we built our values and vision upon. It was incredibly thrilling to then see it come alive with our first letter of thanks from a care-home customer! This is what we wake up in the morning to do."

Like anyone setting up in business, Chai didn't know he was going to be successful.

"My experience has been that if I've made a huge effort, generally I've been able to get close to where I've wanted to get to. I've grown up to view every problem as being there to be solved. I've only known you can win. It's not that I haven't had failures but I always remember the successes, and the failures don't seem to stop me wanting to try again.

"If you work in a system all your life where you're made to feel you're a failure and you haven't achieved anything, then everything focuses on what you didn't get done. You grow up fearful of failure and that doesn't allow you to take risks.

"The biggest motivation for people who do their dream job is the opportunity for self-expression. They want to be able to do something they really want to do. They have an idea, a vision.

"In the UK and Europe we're slightly two-dimensional about business people – we think they're in business just to make money. Well, actually, most people are in business not to become millionaires but to do what they want to do and be happy doing it. And money just happens to come if it's successful. People go into business because they want to be in charge of their own destiny. That's why selling a business is very difficult – because it's your baby. There's a lot of emotion involved."

HC-One

When the Southern Cross care home company collapsed in 2010, Chai took it over and created a new healthcare company, HC-One.

"Even though HC-One has been incredibly hard work, I can't remember being this happy in my work life for a long time. This is what I love doing at the end of the day. You go through life sometimes and think, 'Do I know what I really like in life or do I just consume things? When you do something like this, you can see I'm like a child who's got a really great toy.

"The hardest part of this latest venture was working out what to say when I went to the first meeting of the managers. Why are we doing this? Why have we taken this on? When we look back in a year's time what will we see? Creating the possibility to envision a future and that narrative is the hardest part – whether it's a brand new start up, whether you're talking to a bank manager for money, or your first customer. What's different about us? What does it stand for? It's not yet real. You live it out, and as you live it out the story comes alive and you feel, 'I wrote that map – we found that way to that destination.'

"That's the adventure. I would stand up and say, 'Guys, we're going to Tokyo, not New York, but I can't tell you if we're taking a bus, plane or train, and we may go backwards and forwards a couple of times before we get there. But what I can tell you is that we're going to take you.'

"What you make clear is the destination. For us it was about quality service. It's about the individual being important – that's the destination. If it's not good enough for your mum, it's not good enough for me. How we get to that destination from today, we'll make up as we go along."

Philanthropy

Chai wanted to be financially successful, but ultimately that was in order to be able to stop working for money and become involved in philanthropic work. "The millionaire part was how I could fulfil that part of the journey. That's been brilliant because at 50 I wanted to do that and I've changed my life now. I spend my time as much in not-for-profit areas as in profit areas. I spend as much time giving money away as I do making money. Actually I don't think of it as giving it away, I think of it as investing in projects that will give me a return in profit and make an impact on society."

Chai's biggest challenge

"Our biggest challenge was when we nearly went bust at Court Cavendish. Interest rates went from seven percent to 15 percent in two years. I learnt a lot about cash flow and business management in real time. I always think, in any business cycle, if you haven't looked at the abyss once, then you haven't lived! You know you have to go to that dark spot and come back from it. But we kept our humanity together. We didn't do anything hard or harsh along the way."

Chai's Secrets
TO DREAM BUSINESS SUCCESS

"

1 Be clear about what you want to do. Think through the issues in detail. What will it take to achieve what you're doing? Whether you are raising money, finding a partner, whatever it is, make sure your argument is extremely compelling. Don't be put off if someone says no the first time round. Or the second. If you're very clear about what you want to do, just keep at it.

2 Seek out a group of people. We call them mentors now – friends and counsellors who can guide you and help you and keep you motivated when things are not working. And talk to lots of people about what you're doing. Don't be frightened, because the more you talk about it the more real it becomes.

3 Successful entrepreneurs are passionate and driven; they make things happen and love solving problems. They are not put off by the norms of the time and are willing to stand by what they believe in. You have to be courageous.

"

What would Chai have done differently?

"There are one or two conflicts in my life I would have dealt with differently. I've become more measured and thoughtful about how those conflicts could be resolved. But that's the biggest sort of learning curve – managing people."

The key to Chai's success

"I have the obsessional characteristics all entrepreneurs have: the attention to detail, the finishing and completing, the staying up all night to prepare the presentation, the not letting go.

"But I've actually succeeded, more often than not, because I have amazing teams of people that I work with, and they all contribute to the overall success."

COACHING TIPS **#2**

You don't know what you don't know

You don't have to be an alpha guy or gal, a high-fiving graduate of Harvard Business School or an extrovert who can open doors with one flash of your winning smile and hand-crushing handshake to be a successful entrepreneur. In fact, in some businesses uber-self-confidence and salesy pushiness could play against you.

When thinking about your dream business it is a good idea to do a values inventory. Values are the blueprint of our Self – they are the things we trust, believe in and which resonate with us at a deep level. Grace, family, magnificence, to serve, educate, lead, inspire, solve, direct, enlighten, amuse, charm, dominate, excel, rare, traditional, advanced, ethical, magic, to heal – these are just a few examples of values. Take some time out to identify what values you stand for and aim to bring these into your business to reflect your brand.

The destination for Chai's business reflected his values: quality service and the paramount importance of the individual – if it's not good enough for your mum, it's not good enough for him. Knowing what you and your business represent will run through your enterprise like a stick of rock, from your logo and branding through to your customer service and how you deliver. Like attracts like, so if you know your values, like-minded customers will recognise that and gravitate towards your message. It's like coming home.

If you have had little or no experience running a business (and surprisingly few have who start out), now is the time to research and investigate. Who is doing something similar to what you have in mind? Can you explore how they do it and learn from them?

Mistakes

A big mistake when starting a business is to be the jack of all trades and in a bid to save money try to run every part of the business. But truly successful entrepreneurs play to their core strength, the real reason they went into business, be it decorating cakes or designing advanced software.

Spending your limited time and energy doing things you are not good at will be a self-defeating waste of resources and in the long run money. So plan to outsource as soon as you are financially able.

Outsourcing

Find a bookkeeper who deals with small start-ups. Hire a VA (virtual assistant) who is happy to work by the hour to send and chase invoices, plan your diary, redirect your phone calls, sort techie problems, arrange meetings and make difficult phone calls for you.

There are companies that will undertake your cold sales calls, conduct market research, answer and process orders and deliveries, and there are legions of highly qualified graduates and interns who will work on an hourly rate for the experience.

No one can be expected to be the accountant, secretary, technical support and sales person as well as CEO of their own business. These investments in outsourcing allow you do to what you do best and keep the vision alive.

Business training

If necessary, invest in webinars, teleclasses, weekend courses in accounting, marketing, website optimisation and PR to learn new skills which will help your business until you can afford to pay someone else to do them. Many businesses allow you the chance to train on the job or via home study courses.

You may be surprised to learn that few people in business are MBA graduates and the most successful, like Lord Sugar, Richard Branson, Karren Brady and Jamie Oliver, for example, didn't gain their business prowess by taking business-oriented degrees.

It is entirely possible to start your business with the know-how you currently have and building your business knowledge as you progress.

Probably the single most effective way to learn how to develop good business practice is to join some business networking groups or hire a coach to help you grow and learn on the job.

It's a good idea to 'moonlight' whilst in paid employment to see if your business idea has legs. You can create an inexpensive website or business Facebook page, get a market stall, or piggy-back someone else's business by offering your goods or services under their umbrella. Associates and affiliates are a great way of getting your services out there without huge financial cost.

You're going to need a bigger boat

Most people balk at the idea of creating a business plan; they tap their heads with a knowing "It's all up here." Yes, it's great to have a clear focus on your dream but it is vital to have a well-documented one if you wish to attract investors or get a loan.

You can do a one-year or five-year business plan, and it should include financial forecasts, marketing and sales strategies, management and staff proposals and growth and opportunity predictions. There are many companies that can help you write your business plan, but for a good starting point visit Business Link (businesslink.gov.uk), where you can download various templates.

You could also create a vision board for your business with images of success to inspire you on a daily basis – use this as a golden carrot to keep you motivated and in motion.

CHAPTER 3

Money:

Knowing your worth

66 I visualise the bigger picture the whole time…
I was really struck by the banking crisis. I
wondered who had visualised the bigger
picture. I've always worked on the very
simple basis (because I have a simple mind):
more [money] in than out is quite helpful. 99

Cath Kidston
Desert Island Discs,
BBC Radio 4, 1 May 2011

Passion is what gets you past the difficult bits. But what I love is earning money. That's also what drives me – not just doing it from a place of lack – but from a passion for earning.

Antonia Chitty

I LOVE Antonia's story because it shows the challenges that working mothers face – juggling two roles, trying to be in two places at once – and how they can be overcome in an entirely sensible, straightforward, practical way. Despite having no business background, Antonia wasn't put off from setting up on her own. She learnt on the way. For those who want to earn a good income and work flexibly on your own terms, this story is for you. It's an excellent template for how to start your dream business.

DREAM BUSINESS OWNER

Antonia Chitty
Co-founder,
ACE Inspire, UK

JOURNEY

Eye-care professional ➡ Journalist, author and UK Mumpreneur of the Year

From optometry to PR

Antonia chose a 'sensible' working career as an optometrist, because she was good at science and writing. When she actually started work she found the job highly repetitive and eventually got bored by it. "I worked in optometry for five years before moving to the Royal National Institute for the Blind, doing PR. They wanted someone with eye knowledge to promote their charity." She then worked for *Which* magazine, writing health features.

But it was the birth of her first baby that forced Antonia to take a career break and reassess her working life.

"I thought maternity leave wasn't that interesting and wanted to return to work. So I got a new job working for the British Medical Association. It provided a good pay rise but when I had my baby and went back to work it just wasn't doing it for me.

"I didn't feel I was doing a great job at the BMA, and I had to leave at 5 pm to pick my daughter up from nursery. I wasn't doing a good job being a mum either, because I had to keep going to work! And a substantial part of my salary was being spent paying for her to be looked after."

The lightbulb moment

"I had one phone call with a life coach and she showed me that if I put everything together I actually had lots of skills, and that meant that I could work for myself. I had skills people would pay for. That was my lightbulb moment. So I got off the phone with her and decided I was going to do feature writing. I pitched a couple of features to a trade publication where I had a contact and they said, 'Yes, lovely, write them.'

"I thought it was going to be really good. However, I ended up doing more PR than feature writing because feature writing requires a substantial amount of time pitching to get your articles taken up, whereas with PR I found people were coming to me. So I went with the flow."

Antonia decided to take the plunge and hand in her notice at the

BMA. During her notice period she set up her website in the evenings after putting her daughter to bed.

"I also signed up for a course with our local enterprise centre, which was very helpful and provided a quick headstart. The other thing that was enormously helpful was joining forums where there were other working parents – people who'd been doing it for slightly longer than me. It was really a place where, if I hit a problem, there would be someone else who'd hit the problem before and could help me. So I spent a lot of the first couple of years asking people who'd been there and done that, making the most of their experience.

"I did do a business plan. That's really valuable. I'm always telling people to make plans. A plan makes you think, 'Where do I want to go? Where's this business heading?' And if you don't know where the business is heading, it's very hard to have any direction. Any plan, unless you update it, pretty much becomes out of date as soon as you start doing business because reality is always different."

As well as making a business plan, Antonia carried out market research. This included linking up with people online and finding out what they wanted. It also enabled her to find out about prices.

Pricing

"I discovered that I'd pitched my prices way too low, so I revised them. I learnt a lot in the first few years of running that business and a lot of it was by trial and error. However good my business plan was to start off with, nothing beats doing it in reality.

If you're stuck at the stage of thinking 'I'd like to start a business' – well, just get out there, make a prototype, hold a market stall, find somebody who'd like to try your service. Get people to give you real feedback on what you're actually going to offer and check that it's the right thing at the right price. That way the customer is happy and you're getting the right amount of money for the hours you put in."

Antonia's first customer was Robina from *Optometry Today*, who commissioned her to write a feature. And her first PR customer was a lady in Wales who made cloth nappies.

"I needed to do some market research, so we did a trade-off whereby I wrote a press release for her and she sent me a set of cloth nappies for my daughter. I did a trade-off for my website too. Then I did some PR for a lady who was setting up her own website design business, and she set up my site for me. So there was a lot of trading to get me up and running and a lot of feedback from people.

"Luckily, I had some happy customers before I started spreading the word more widely. One of the key things I did at that stage was realise that not everyone could pay me to do the PR for them. So I started writing a series of fact sheets which I also made available."

Developing a product

"I showed the fact sheets to a couple of people and one of my clients. They all said they were really good, and that I should make them into a book. So I knew the market was out there. Thus, as well as offering my services by the hour, I was developing a product to sell. If you've got a service business you've also got to develop a product."

Having a book published made a real difference to the way people perceived Antonia. Not only did it increase the opportunities for speaking but she got a regular booking training at the very same place she'd trained in business herself a few years before. It also meant she had a product to sell at live events and via her website.

"It was there for people who would call me up to talk about doing PR work and then say they didn't have the budget. I was able to say, 'Fine, if you want to do it yourself rather than get me to do it for you, here's the book.' It really did hit the mark on a lot of levels."

A new direction

During her third pregnancy, Antonia found a new direction. "I was quite ill so I had to sit around, which got me into blogging and doing much more development on the Family Friendly Working website. I'd created the blog in order to publicise my book, but now I started getting an income from the blog – through advertising and a directory where people could pay to post. And building on the resources in the book, I could then add in relevant and useful things for working parents on the blog."

Antonia realised that her income didn't have to depend on the hours she put in. She could generate a passive income. She wrote another book, *The Mumpreneur Guide*, in which she shared her experience of setting up with other mums who wanted to start a business. It was designed for them to put in their handbags and consult at odd moments like while waiting to collect the kids from nursery.

"However, with a young family and a very small baby, I knew I wasn't going to be able to do all the promotion for the book myself. That was another breakthrough. It might be that you can do things but that doesn't necessarily mean you are the best person to do them. So Lindsey Collumbell at Bojangle Communications worked with me over a six-month period, and she gave the book a very good launch.

"At the same time, I won the first Inspirational Business Mum of the Year award at the Mumpreneur Conference. So although I was thinking the business wasn't working in one way, there were all these other opportunities that were giving me a real shove to say, 'No, maybe your business shouldn't just be about doing PR for other people. Maybe your business is more about getting other mums into business.'"

A passion for earning

Antonia is refreshing in her attitude to money. "Passion is what gets you past the difficult bits. But what I love is earning money. That's also what drives me – not just doing it from a place of lack, but from a passion for earning."

Her achievement is all the greater because she has stringent time constraints. "I have got limitations – but I'm going to succeed anyway. I'm going to do it on my own terms and this is one of the reasons why I want to help other women set up their own businesses. It's about not being held back by 'the system.'

"When I was working what I thought were relatively flexible hours with quite a good employer, I still didn't feel I spent enough time with my daughter. Flexible working is not going to work for every mum. If anyone's ever thought about having to pay nursery fees for more than one child and said, 'There's got to be another way,' or whose boss has said they can't go to the school play because it doesn't fit with their working hours – it's those things that drive me to say, 'Yes, you *can* do it.' And right now the passion we have is for saying to women, you don't have to have a small business, you don't have to have a business that only pays pocket money. You can dream big. Through ACE Inspire, we help women to take small businesses and turn them into medium businesses and then bigger businesses."

What would Antonia have done differently?

"It's brilliant now working with a business partner. It would have been nicer to do that sooner, but you can't just magic the right person out of nowhere. You need to have a wide network to find that person. But maybe I could have considered the option earlier on. A lot of what I've done has been essential to the process of learning."

Antonia's inspiration

"Jo Fairley, the founder of Green & Black's chocolates. She has written books and owns the Wellington Centre for holistic wellness and a bakery. She's juggling her career running the chocolate business and the bakery but she's still writing. That's multitasking and that makes me think I could learn from her."

Antonia's attitude to the recession

"For ACE Inspire, the recession has given us a lot of opportunities. A lot of people are saying they need to think of a different way to work. ACE Inspire is all about helping people train so that they can work in a flexible way that fits around their family. I think the recession hasn't made it easier, but for those who've got the courage to start a business in a recession the only way is up.

"I've been doing it long enough to know that not everything's going to go wrong at once. I've got a business that's got a fairly big income base. Which is great – if money comes in from one thing one month and another thing another month, that's fine. At ACE Inspire, Erica Douglas and I regularly ask what's bringing in the money and what's not? What will we get rid of? We've only got a limited number of hours in the day. We don't want to spend all of those hours working. You have to ask yourself what is the most profitable activity – OK, let's do more of that!"

How important is social networking to Antonia?

"Vital. I really couldn't do what I do without the internet, right from those first days when I met up with other women via a work-at-home forum and started doing trades to get my business online. Very few of my clients were ever local – they were mostly people I'd met online. Twitter and Facebook were just the things that I was waiting for to grow the business. I've got a really good online network which enables me to live in a slightly out-of-the-way little town and still have the business that I've got."

Antonia's biggest challenge

"Having three children. When you've got three children you don't have time to be hitting the phones, making the phone calls you need to make in PR. So I had to have a big rethink at that stage. A lot of business owners find they hit a ceiling, particularly if they're in a service business where you just can't put any more hours in."

Antonia's biggest success

"The *Mumpreneur Guide* coming out at the same time as my winning the Inspirational Business Mum award. It coincided with my having six months out and not being able to do anything very much. More recently *Blogging: The Essential Guide* has been an enormous success. It got into Amazon's Top 250 list and won product of the month on MumsClub. It all helps make you feel that it's working!

"But perhaps my success is more personal than that. I think I've learnt over the years what makes me tick, and how to pool all my skills together in a way that's fulfilling. When I was 16 and choosing my career I was listening to what other people said, but now I know what works for me. I think I've done as much learning about myself over the last ten years as I have learning about business strategies! And I probably wouldn't have started doing that if I hadn't had postnatal depression. The depression was a result of having everything familiar to me – getting up, going to work,

Antonia's Secrets
TO DREAM BUSINESS SUCCESS

66

1 Have a plan. You've got to know where you're heading. If you have a final destination in mind you have a better chance of reaching it.

2 Persevere. A lot of people think, 'I wish I could be as successful as so-and-so,' but generally the people who stand out as successes are those who have stuck at it.

3 Promote. Have ongoing promotions – just one thing every day to put the word out about your business. That's where my background has really helped me. It's alright to tell people about your business.

4 Get some support. If you can, join a networking group; find other people who are doing something similar locally. Get a mentor, or a coach – then you've always got someone to go to when you hit that 'I don't know what to do.'

5 When setting up, ask yourself, 'Do people need this, and want it, and have the money to pay for it?' It's easy to set up a business just because you want to – that's important, of course, but it shouldn't be the only thing. Do your market research: many people say they need something but then it turns out they don't really want to pay for it, or they'll see if they can get it cheaper elsewhere – or free!

99

doing work in an environment you can be in control of – replaced with being on my own looking after a small child. Babies are unpredictable and you can't control them. And I really struggled with that to start off with. It made me look at who I was and put me back together in a new form that I'm much happier with."

COACHING TIPS #3

Show me the money, honey

Let's face it, we all have issues around money. You may have a 'deficit' mindset, where you feel you never have enough, an 'ostrich' mindset, where you bury your head in the sand around invoices and debts, or a 'status' mindset, where you feel defined by your bank balance.

Whatever the case, the bottom line is you need to manage your beliefs around wealth to ensure your business is profitable and abundant.

How not to undersell yourself – setting your rate card

If you have any hangups about charging what you are worth, it will be you who stands in the way of your business success. Charging what you are worth means you value and honour your products and services, it means you regard them highly and, by association, you and your company have healthy self-esteem. Others will identify with this and will pay you and respect what you do accordingly.

If you start undercutting, slashing prices or find yourself being knocked down by a difficult client or because of fear, then you can feel resentful and this will show up in how you treat your business and services.

Chances are the client could also turn out to be not the loyal or raving fan your business needs but a difficult and demanding one.

So set your rate card and hold your nerve. You can't easily go back to full rate once you have come down on your prices. And be prepared to put your prices up annually. It is important not to make assumptions about the market. Check what your competitors charge and then decide where you fit in. Are you the top luxury end of things? Mid-market? Budget but good value?

If you want to charge more, how can you add extra value that won't cost you more? You could consider small giveaways, reports, the way you deliver services, follow-up, customer care, personalised service, unusual packaging, loyalty discounts, membership offers – all these things add value, make you stand out and keep you ahead of your competitors.

You can flag up the benefits of using you – what your USP is – with the confidence that you provide a good service and charge accordingly. If the price tag is low and you don't trust your own abilities, you will attract people who pick up on this message, people who want the lowest rate regardless of quality and service. This could eventually give you and your business a bad name.

Dangerous assumptions

Sometimes it is OK to develop special prices or packages for individuals but beware of your assumptions about your customers and clients.

I once coached a nutritionist who received a phone call from a potential new client, a banker, who was interested in her services. He asked how much the initial introductory session was and she said £25. He didn't hear it clearly, so she repeated, "Two five," to which he said, "Only £25? I thought it was £250. I don't want it then."

Sometimes people *want* to pay more. How cool is that? This client wanted 'reassuringly expensive' and there is a market for that too.

Equally we can make assumptions about clients or customers that can be entirely wrong. You may even project onto them your own story, e.g. "These clients look poor / I pity them / I think I'd better make an exception here / I want them to like me – they look powerful and connected, they might bring me more business."

Then because you set up a deficit assumption about them you may then treat them differently from your other full-paying clients. Then, horror of horrors, you find they own oil wells in Saudi Arabia! Then how do you feel?

It's key that you have professional boundaries around you and your rate card. When you truly value your expertise, your products and your excellence, your confidence grows and so does the trust of other people.

Toolbox tips

- Do you truly believe in what you do?

- Is there a confidence deficit in yourself and your business?

- How is charging little serving you?

- What fear is behind it?

- When you charge what you are worth, you feel rewarded, and your clients treat you and your services with respect.

Overcoming sales fear and resistance

We all experience a stab of fear when closing a sale or naming a price or submitting a proposal for future work. Was it too much and that's why they are not responding? I daren't call them and follow up. Have I charged too little and that's why they were so quick to sign up?

It's important you establish your price structure and how much you are willing to be flexible. Equally it is vital from the outset that you have firm terms and conditions in place. These explain how you work, how you get paid and by when. Ensure your clients are aware of these from the outset.

Now comes the most important part – establishing rock-hard personal and professional boundaries, e.g. you won't go below a certain price, you demand punctuality in payment, and clients must respect your time (no calls in the evenings or at weekends – or if so, you must have an out-of-hours rate).

We all need to firm up our boundaries in work and let go of people-pleasing.

We have looked at some fears around charging what you are worth:

- I have priced myself out of the market.

- People won't buy.

- I may not be good enough for this price tag.

- I feel mean charging that much.

Now think about the reverse of your fears with these mantras:

- I provide a superb service.

- I am value for money.

- You won't get better than what I offer.

- I have proven results.

- People are impressed with what I do and are happy to pay.

- I add value.

- I deserve this.

- I am worth it.

Do what you have to do to believe these statements. Your competitors do it. You must too.

CHAPTER 4

New kids on the block

"Supermarkets are notorious for not answering the phone, hanging up on you and not wanting to deal with small companies. Nobody would answer my phone calls and they all laughed when I said I was a barrister. So I got in my car with my sauces, six weeks after leaving law and starting the business, and I drove to Bracknell.

I went to reception and asked for the buyer. I said, 'Is Laura here? She's not answered my phone calls. Can I speak to her?' They called her and because it was an internal call from reception she picked up. She asked me to leave the sauces in reception but I said, 'No! They're fresh, they're chilled, they'll go off. I've come all the way to meet you.'

So I got her downstairs, looked her in the eyes, shook her hand, smiled and made friends with her in five minutes. The next day they agreed to have my sauces in 400 stores across Waitrose. That is what you need. That is what it takes to be an entrepreneur.

It's very easy to say no to an email, it's very easy not to respond, but it's really hard for a human being to look another human being in the eye and say no."

Priya Lakhani
Founder of Masala Masala

People told me, 'You'll never do it,' 'Nothing's changed in baby food for years.'

Paul Lindley

P AUL LINDLEY RUNS one of the most successful companies in the UK, organic baby food brand, Ella's Kitchen. Paul started from scratch, knowing nothing about supply chains or supermarkets. His story proves that you can be the new kid on the block and compete with the big boys. Driven by a commitment to tackle childhood obesity, Paul honed and shaped his company to realise his ambitions.

DREAM BUSINESS OWNER

Paul Lindley
Founder,
Ella's Kitchen, UK

JOURNEY

TV production ➡ CEO of organic children's food company

Before embarking on his entrepreneurial journey, Paul trained at KPMG. It quickly became apparent to him, however, that suits, formality and waiting to apply for the next promotion were not how he wanted to spend his life.

"In my early twenties I decided I would get jobs I didn't especially like in order to learn about business, so that in my late twenties I could get jobs I liked – and so that in my thirties I could set up my own business. In other words, I thought in an entrepreneurial way from early on."

Working as an accountant was just one part of that education. The next stage came when Paul joined the children's TV company, Nickelodeon UK. Within ten years, he saw the business and his team grow from 20 employees to 150. It was, by then, a leading brand and Paul had overseen every aspect of the business development – from revenue to subscription, brand development and TV operations.

Paul's time at Nickelodeon fed into his awareness of a market that has since developed into a successful business and a passionate campaign – children and their relationship with food.

"I have a passion for children's issues, and I understand children as consumers of goods and services. I was looking to fill a gap in the market, a social need.

"I was ready for a challenge. At Nickelodeon we had carried out research and focus groups with children and it was an excellent grounding in how they think.

"I was aware of children's health and social issues – 30 percent of children are overweight. Watching television had been blamed for this – all that inactivity plus the adverts for unhealthy foods."

The camping holiday

"My business idea came together during a camping holiday in 2004. I had tried to find convenient and healthy food to pack for my daughter Ella and son Paddy but I couldn't find any. There was a gap in the market. Why didn't I plug that gap?

"Within a day I had taken my wife through it. She was as interested in me satisfying my entrepreneurial needs as I was. So we made it a family enterprise by naming the business after our daughter. We wanted the brand to have an 'authenticity' – after all, it's an authentic problem and we have a real family.

"It doesn't take ten years working in the industry to know that television has mass reach and mass impact. I knew it was key and I knew how it worked. Often there aren't enough adverts to fill the space. I was a start-up and needed to be creative with how I spent my capital, so, thinking differently, I offered a share of the revenue instead of advertising fees to Nickelodeon.

"If the product was successful it would ultimately provide significant added revenue for the TV company. If it wasn't, I didn't pay. So within the first six weeks, Viacom, who owns Nickelodeon, broadcast our adverts under this new idea of revenue-sharing. It was an innovative approach but it worked out well."

The brand

"I gave myself two years to develop a brand that would be innovative enough to go directly into the UK supermarkets. I didn't want to trial in the local farm shops, because I wanted to make a real difference to children's health and therefore I knew I had to build the brand quickly and be trusted.

"Products can be copied very quickly and manufactured more cheaply by the big boys. But we were different. It was about creating an innovative product of fantastic quality. We created something that was cool and fun for the children – so it would appeal to them. But it was also healthy, which appealed to adults and parents like me. Up to this point the marketing of baby products had been aimed at the parents.

"I was very excited. I thought, if I don't do this now I'll regret it for the rest of my life. I'd been working for fifteen years and I was at a stage where I could afford to take a risk. I knew there would be no holidays, but I didn't want to be reading a book like this about someone else having done it. My fear of regret outweighed my fear of the risk.

"I really believe individuals can make a difference, and that continued to drive me. If we don't do something about the trend of poor childhood health, parents outliving their children will be the natural course of events. This business fitted with the social angle."

The product

"Whilst I knew about marketing to kids and I had a family and cooked for my children at home, I knew nothing about manufacturing or supply chains."

Paul conducted research and took advice from paediatricians and nutritionists. He had a big decision to make about the food production: Should he manufacture the products himself or should he outsource? Manufacturing would have required more capital investment. He decided to outsource, working on the basis that he should focus on the bits he did know and allow other experts to take the lead on the aspects he didn't.

"I worked on my own for 18 months just trying to set up the business and brand proposition. Financially, I was on target, spending £25,000. This funded experts and the artwork. Finding the correct buyer and the right person to talk to was the hardest thing.

"Getting that first order was my biggest challenge. Setting up a meeting required between 50 and 100 phone calls to even get their interest. They never rang back and my background was not in sales."

New kid on the block

"I approached Tesco, Sainsbury's, Waitrose and Boots. They were in the process of category reviews which meant they were changing their shelves for new stock. I had meetings and pitched to them.

"Once I got a buyer on the phone I would tell them how we were different and why it would work. I demonstrated my passion, insight and belief that children were consumers in their own right.

"Then, my first sale came in. Sainsbury's said they were interested and would get back to me; the waiting game ensued. So much was hanging in the balance. A second week passed and I'd heard nothing. And someone else had got back to say, 'Not on this occasion.' I was beginning to run out of options."

On the third week of waiting, Paul picked up a voicemail message from the Sainsbury's buyer who said they wanted to launch the company in January in 350 stores across the UK.

"The initial elation lasted for 30 seconds. After that the realisation hit me that now I had to actually do it. Up to that point I hadn't sold anything to anyone. By chance the buyer was a mum and fitted our demographic.

"It was just as Sainsbury's was launching its 'Buy Something New Today' campaign. Ella's Kitchen was going to be one of the new products. They kicked off with Smoothie Fruits. It was very different. It was convenience food but less processed."

Sainsbury's gave Paul 12 weeks to prove Ella's Kitchen could sell.

Delivery

"We remortgaged the house. I didn't want to sell equity. We'd been given this opportunity and we wanted to control and develop it ourselves but I remained confident. Outsourcing the manufacture had been the right decision."

Since then, Ella's Kitchen has grown tremendously quickly, to become a business with 57 employees and a £50 million turnover. In June 2010 they were voted Food Brand of the Year, beating other finalists (including Hovis, Cadbury and Walkers). Ella's Kitchen now makes 77 products, and every second of every day someone around the world is eating an Ella's product.

"This is all a testament to getting it right. We've got a 15 percent supermarket share in the UK, a US subsidiary now, and operate in 12 markets around the world. The personal journey for me has been making a difference to the children's food market. We've done it by being innovative and thinking differently.

"I like to think I have created an uncorporate company. It's open, like a family of people who like to work together. Ella's Kitchen is my third child, really.

"It's a very personal brand. By doing this I feel I have lived up to myself. You live one life, and for me it's about trying lots of different things. People told me, 'You'll never do it,' 'Nothing's changed in baby food for years,' 'They won't take you seriously.' But things can be done. There's that quote by J.F. Kennedy, 'Some men see things as they are and ask why... I dream of things that never were and ask why not.' If someone says to me there's a 99 percent chance that something can't be done – to me that means there's a one percent chance it can be done. If you think like that, that's your point of difference."

What does Paul wish he'd known before he started?

"I wish I'd known how much hard work it really is. I now realise I was a one-man band for too long. A passionate team not only shares the workload and creates new ideas but generates motivation and ultimately – if you get it right – comes to work because of the values the brand lives by and the sense of purpose it gives them and the exciting journey they help drive. It's important to keep my team motivated so the staff can do what they've been employed to do with a smile."

Paul's attitude to social media

"For our brand, social media is very important. Our target demographic spends a lot of time online. We have launched an Ella's Friends database, which now has well over 100,000 parents on it;

Paul's Secrets

TO DREAM BUSINESS SUCCESS

66

1 Be focused.

2 Know why you're different.

3 Know why you're doing it.

4 Know where there's a market gap.

5 Do your research. Understand your consumer. What's he or she saying?

6 Make sure your financial numbers stack up. Have a business plan that works where the funding is sensible with clever ways of minimising need for money. Is the business sustainable?

7 Avoid poor cash flow.

8 Be passionate.

9 People skills are essential. Staff need to be valued and rewarded. Know how they contribute. If you have the right people, the world's your oyster, so it's important to keep them and motivate them.

99

we've got over 30,000 likes on Facebook and around 5000 followers on Twitter. We want to be a trusted brand, so it makes sense for us to give customers a forum to talk about all aspects of how they see our brand and products.

"We can then respond to any praise or criticism. Without that, if someone doesn't like something then it's out in the ether. If we provide a forum for that feedback, it is more controllable and adds value to our brand and product development."

I am quite easygoing – that's important because when you run a business you're going to have lots of challenges. You need to have a calm nature.

Horr Wai Wong

IN THIS next entrepreneurial snapshot, Malaysian business owner Horr Wai Wong set up two businesses when he saw a gap in the market. With a passion for running businesses as well as for IT, he is currently working on a third business – developing an app.

Since studying commerce and law at Melbourne University, Horr Wai

DREAM BUSINESS OWNER

Horr Wai Wong
Founder,
Sports Planet, Sports Tech Pro, and Adgoggle, Malaysia

JOURNEY

Corporate employee ➡
Multiple entrepreneur

always knew he wanted to have his own business. He started
working for Anderson Consulting Kuala Lumpur and while
he was with them he was contacted by a friend who wanted to
start up internet-based companies. They began to work together,
but Horr Wai also started his own futsal (indoor football)
venue company.

"I had worked for four years and felt I wanted to start out on my
own. I was looking for a business to run. At that time there was
only one sports venue open, so I went with my friend to see what
it was like. It was very crowded! There was so much demand, and
not enough pitches. In Malaysia the English Premier League is
very popular on television. I called up another friend and asked
if he had any warehouses available that I could use. He found me
one and I opened my own futsal court in it."

Horr Wai found more venues, and each time he bought sports
flooring from a local supplier. "I knew this guy quite well and
I called and suggested we start a company and start supplying
sports floorings both to my venues and to other people as well.
He had all the know-how to select and install the floorings. We
started off small but now we have the whole range of sports
floorings – we can put down football pitches, hockey fields,
tennis courts. The business has been growing every year since
we started.

"That was just an opportunity that came along. I asked myself,
instead of buying in so much flooring, why didn't I set up my
own?"

The next venture

Horr Wai is restless – he's not content with two companies, he wants more! "Since last year I've had a bit of time on my hands because these two companies of mine have teams of people running them. I give them guidance and try to push them along. But I've been feeling that I should try and do something else.

"I have a passion for IT and I think it's very scalable. In my futsal venues, once the courts are fully booked you can't book more people. But with one server you can serve 1000 people. Mobile advertising is growing very rapidly so I'm developing an app. It's still in the very early stages.

"There are risks to starting up new ventures, but there are ways that you can go about it that minimise the risk. Don't quit your job right away – get your start-up going first. There will come a time when you need to commit in order to focus, but some of the initial preparation can definitely be done while you're at work."

Horr Wai's biggest success

"Sports Planet has been around for ten years and is still going and is a stable, profitable company. The sports flooring company has seen a lot of growth."

Impact of the recession

"So far the businesses have been recession-proof. Futsal is not an expensive activity at $8 per person and so even with the downturn in the economy people are still playing."

Horr Wai's keys to being successful

"When you face a wall that is stopping you from reaching your destination, you can stand there and just wait or you can try climbing over it. Or breaking through it. Eventually you will solve the problem – you've got to be creative. If you're flogging a dead horse, don't waste your time. But don't give up easily; keep trying until you find a way.

"You mustn't get too emotional in business. Say you have a disagreement with your business partner. You need to be able to sit down and discuss, and come to an understanding. Both of you need to be calm and reasonable."

Advice to a new kid on the block

"I like mountain biking, hiking and outdoor activities. A friend of mine sells camping stuff online – bags, knives and camping equipment. He's been doing this business for a year and now he wants to open a shop. He wants to open up in one of my venues that is in a very good location with a lot of people coming in. I agreed but asked to be a shareholder because I have a passion for outdoor activities. So I put in the capital in proportion to my shareholder percentage. We came to an agreement that we would probably have the shop in January. What I think he needs to do is get enough capital for stock. He needs to work out how much stock he needs to buy in order to sell; how much money he needs to renovate the shop; how much to cover his costs for six months. Then he needs to have a forecast by looking at his sales online and working out what he can improve."

COACHING TIPS #4
Going the distance

When interviewed for Desert Island Discs and asked about the good fortune in his life, business leader Lord Digby Jones said, "The harder I work the luckier I get."

Many of us starting our own businesses often fall into the trap of thinking there must be some golden key out there that if turned will magically bring abundance flowing into our bank accounts. We assume we must be missing something and start taking up extra evening or online courses to be sure.

Sometimes we might invest in some expensive new gadget or marketing offer that promises the deliverance of wealth; other times we just think that some people have been given a bucket to dip into the sea of success while we were given a teaspoon with a hole in it.

This way of thinking presupposes that there is always something just out of grasp, something unseen that needs to be accessed.

But the real route to success comes down to hard work, tenacity and a steely belief in what you are doing. Being a business person means you have to be positive, upbeat and ready to drive your services or products at all times. It takes heaps of energy and confidence that it will pay off even when the chips are down and times feel tough.

As we have seen from this chapter, Paul Lindley made up to 100 phone calls before Sainsbury's agreed to trial his range of baby food.

This is not unusual. It isn't easy and it takes a lot of nerve to maintain one's dynamism in the face of rejection, indifference or disregard. If Horr Wai Wong faces a wall, he thinks creatively to get round it, through it or over it.

Failure isn't fatal

When the going gets tough don't throw in the towel. Take the time to refocus and take stock of what you have learned.

If at first you don't succeed, you have several options:

- Step back and reassess. Give yourself some time off, to clear your mind and get 'distance' and a fresh perspective.

- Strategically network. Find specialist networking groups in fields relevant to what you do and be sure to dynamically spread your message.

- Visit large trade shows and see what's up and coming in your field. Gather information and be curious about what's out there. This isn't a time for raging envy.

- Don't be set in stone. Have the courage to adapt and reshape your concept if need be.

- Ask for constructive feedback and be big enough to accept it and rework your idea or strategy.

- Practise 'selling' your concept to a complete stranger, and listen to possible objections.

Don't be like the gold miner who bought all the expensive mining gear and finally gave up when he was but an inch from hitting a deep seam. You never know what is around the corner.

Coaching questions

- What is working well at the moment? What do you need to do more of?

- What would a good lead look like to you, and have you told others too?

- Have you precisely focused on what it is you wish to achieve?

- What do you need to get there?

- How long are you prepared to give it?

- How can you change your attitude and energy to make this work?

- You head says… but your heart says…?

We have all encountered down days, disappointments, naysayers and frustrations. Even highly successful people. But the difference between the successful and those who fail is that the former don't let the negative hold them back.

Your choice.

CHAPTER 5

Developing the millionaire mindset

"True success is about hanging on when everyone else lets go.**"**

Karren Brady

"Sometimes through adversity you find uniqueness – it's not always money that will help you. Having the ability to find a way forward is key to being successful."

Deborah Mitchell

I TOLD some of Deborah Mitchell's story in an earlier book (*Find Your Dream Job*), but that was merely the story of how she changed career and found the job of her dreams. What it didn't tell was the story of her subsequent success as the director of her own company. Deborah epitomises a positive mindset and fully believes that through an optimistic outlook you can achieve whatever success you desire. She is living proof.

DREAM BUSINESS OWNER

Deborah Mitchell
Director, Heaven Health & Beauty Ltd, UK

JOURNEY

Drama student ➡ Founder of organic skincare company

Deborah has built a multimillion-pound beauty product empire. And she has won several prestigious awards, which have helped raise her profile in the UK and internationally. Indeed, her Heaven Bee Venom Mask, a "natural alternative to botox," won a Women in Business Gold Stevie Award for best product. Heaven has taken the market by storm and enjoyed record growth of almost 300 percent in the past year.

And she started out with nothing more than £10 and a burning desire to transform the industry.

Magical thinking

It all started as a kind of magical thinking. Deborah is an ordinary girl from Wolverhampton. She was meant to be taking a class in beauty therapy, but in fact she was staring out the window. She wasn't day-dreaming, she was concentrating on a fully formed vision she had of herself running her own business, her own beauty salons.

She pursued that vision. Whilst still training as a beauty therapist, she started looking for work before the other students to get ahead of the game, giving herself the best chance possible of getting a job in a competitive field. She was hired at a local salon and gained invaluable experience.

After three years she moved to a salon in Wolverhampton. She acquired more experience and eventually left to pursue her grand masterplan of setting up a mobile business.

From the outset, Deborah looked for ways to expand her business and accumulate skills and experience. By investing in a box of nail extensions, she learnt to do nails, which brought in money to do other things.

Whilst it always sounds easy in hindsight, Deborah had plenty of hurdles. She split up from her first husband, but she didn't give up; instead in the same week she opened her first shop in Shropshire.

"I'd set up in a health club, but I had so many clients that I needed new premises and a base to work from."

Over time she built up a team of beauticians to cope with demand. Her reputation continued to grow by word of mouth and she opened a second shop, this time in central London.

A high street chain wanted to manufacture Deborah's products in their factories, but such is her integrity and commitment to making pure, natural products, Deborah opted to remain independent. She went on to a take huge financial risk by buying her own factory and incurred major debt in the process. This was in order to ensure the production of beauty treatments that are genuinely organic and preservative-free. She is driven by a desire to spread healing of the skin, not sell out and jeopardise the quality of the product.

"The way I do business is always the same. It never changes. I never go after the money, I go after looking after people. I make sure the products fit the person in the right way. I don't need to do it any other way. That is my life. That is my passion."

In the past Deborah worried about cash flow and how to pay staff wages, but she doesn't worry now.

"I've just signed a £100 million contract with China and we're selling in Japan and America. Money's not a problem anymore. My life's great, actually. Whether I go up or down from this, I'm still doing what I want to do at the end of the day."

The wheel gets bigger

Deborah now has 85 staff worldwide, so she is responsible for more wages.

"I'm still not really driven by money but I do have to make people's wages. So in fact as my business grows the wheel gets bigger and there's more to earn. I think that you get what you ask for – you just have to ask intelligently. You mustn't doubt whatever it is you want, but you have to work out *what* you want."

People help to promote Deborah's business on her behalf by talking about the products. It helps, of course, that she is now the beauty therapist of choice for many A-list celebrities and members of the royal family. Deborah loves people and people love her.

"I don't have to do Google ads. People just talk about the treatments because they like them and like the products. The clientele that I've got is all sorts of people. When you have a clientele they all talk to one another and to their friends. And in the royal echelons, they talk to everybody. They just happen to be lords and ladies, or Cheryl Cole and Sylvester Stallone! That's what seems to happen. My clients are proud of it and they want to talk about it. They like the fact that the products are all organic."

Major events include the opening of a flagship store in Taiwan as part of a distribution deal in the Far East, followed by a more recent contract in which Deborah's products expect to sell in 2500 Heaven salons in China. As a result of these deals, Deborah has trained hundreds of British therapists to work in the new Chinese stores. Her success has been extraordinary.

"I can't cope with the demand for everything I've got now. But I've got set rules about how I work and what I want to do. I want to carry on treating people. It's something that's really important to me. I did treatments all day yesterday without a break. And I'll be working through to 7.30 tonight with no break. I'm booked up for a year, and really I would be booked up solid for ever if we opened bookings beyond the year!"

Deborah's story is a great one, and truly inspiring to anyone hoping to set up a lucrative dream business.

The mindset

What's her secret? She would say it is a matter of self-belief. "I do believe that if I turn my hand to anything, I can be successful at it. It's not just my knowledge and my experience. I know that if I choose to do it, it will happen and it will work. You make a choice – and a decision. You say, 'I *do* want to do this, and I *do* really want to earn money at it.' People have to make that statement."

But, for me, Deborah's additional secret is her authenticity and her integrity. She is totally committed to organic products and has refused to sell out that dream along the way. Furthermore, she is generous, connects with people and works extremely hard.

She admits to being competitive. She describes herself as a leader but sees herself as a collective leader. "I want my family and my team to be swept along with me. I need to have lots of people around and to pull them along." She is the sole director of her company and doesn't want to share that role because she can't stand people telling her what to do. That has been the case from birth!

Deborah's attitude to social networks

"Social networks are really good. The clue is in the word 'social.' I do it to be social with my mates and thank people for buying the products. But I do get lots of business from it because I engage."

Deborah's biggest challenge

Copying by rival manufacturers has been a problem. When her formulas were stolen one time, she thought she was ruined. But her response was to remake the products into a far superior best-seller. Copycat products are just a part of the challenge of running a successful business. "I try to think there are no setbacks in life, just ways of teaching me things."

Deborah says that juggling family is also amongst her biggest challenges. "You do have to make your commitments to your work and almost book an appointment with relatives to see them, and that is hard."

Deborah's biggest success

"One of my biggest successes is being awarded a fellowship from the college where I used to be called 'Debbie Dumb Blonde.' That feels good!"

The key to Deborah's success

"Actually, I don't think I am successful – yet. But meeting people's requirements is my business and it will be successful because the people I employ care about people."

Deborah's Secrets

TO DREAM BUSINESS SUCCESS

"

1 Focus on what you want to achieve. Ask yourself what you're prepared to sacrifice and how much effort you're prepared to put in. Write it down.

2 When you have your list of what you want, find people to help you achieve each individual thing.

3 If you haven't got a particular skill set, get someone in to give you that skill set.

4 Sometimes you need to choose people on gut instinct. Two years ago a Chinese company and a Taiwanese company were vying for the distribution of my products. The Taiwanese offered to buy £1.37 million of products and give me the money up front. But I turned them down as I didn't feel right about it. I went with the little baby Chinese distributor. And now I've got a £10 million deal with them. They're aiming to open 2500 stores in China. In Japan, the store in Tokyo has attracted the Chelsea Flower Show 2012 gold medal winner Ishihara Kazuyuki to design the garden in it.

5 I'm invited to lots of things but I can't do it all. So I work out which is the best one to go to. Everyone tries to grab every ball – but you don't need to. Be selective.

"

Extreme self-care

Being your own boss is great. You choose the hours, take time off when you want to, and every bit of labour you put in is 100 percent for the benefit of you and your business. Well, that's the theory anyway.

Yes, you choose the hours, so why are you working 14-hour days, seven days a week? Can you remember the last time you gave yourself a weekend off, let alone a proper break? Lunchtimes become a distant memory, you forget what your children and partner look like and the dog runs away when you get home.

Instead of the designer-label-clad, suntanned god or goddess of commerce you thought you were going to be, a grey, tired, anxious-faced ghost looks back at you in the bathroom mirror. Sleep has become allergic to you as you worry about what's still to be done each night and you are beginning to resent holidays because it takes you away from work.

Your waistline looks like the stuff they roll out at Pizza Express and you haven't time to collect your thoughts or your dry cleaning, let alone visit a gym in months. What's going on?

Don't think it won't happen to you. I know one business woman who took her BlackBerry into the delivery room in order to catch up with emails whilst in labour!

It is a sad fact that we can morph into the boss of our worst night-mares; running our own businesses can reduce us to an out-of-shape, overworked bore who talks of nothing else except sales predictions and profit margins.

In order to keep our businesses fresh, alive and healthy, we must be too. If your business hits the buffers, or you're stuck on a plateau where you don't seem to be able to break out of a profit rut, you need to step back and rethink.

Taking time out can seem like a goofing-off guilt trip rather than a brain-clearing investment. We all need to rethink what we are doing in our businesses occasionally and this can be a time to up your training, investigate new options or merely be curious about what else is 'out there.'

Here are some ideas to ensure that all-essential work-life balance, which should keep both you and your business vital and energised.

Toolbox tips

- Set up healthy daily habits – go for a morning walk or run, eat fresh organic produce, drink lots of water, take regular breaks, know when to switch off.

- Create a realistic working day, say 9–6 or 10–7, and stick to it.

- Have non-screen time – shut down the PC, laptop or iPad and stop checking emails on your smartphone at least two hours before bed to allow you to properly unwind.

- Build in NNT time (Non-Negotiable Time) in your diary where you go for a massage, see friends, visit galleries, practise yoga or just stare at a wall.

- Have white space in your diary at least once a week to think, plan and be creative.

- Hire a coach to motivate, inspire, challenge and support you regularly.

- Ensure your office is designed to help you work at your best – up-to-date technology, ergonomic chair, pleasant environment, everything working.

- Have treats to look forward to each day – meals with loved ones, a book at bedtime, a lovely bath, a glass of good wine, an absorbing hobby.

- Learn to meditate – it's a simple technique, and it lowers blood pressure and helps you unwind and refocus.

Coaching questions

- What do you need to help sustain and support you, and help you be at your best? Make a list and action it.

- What toxic habits do you need to zap – e.g. drinking too much caffeine/alcohol, junk food, sugary foods, over-promising, not planning, not being punctual – what needs to change, and how will you do it?

- What support network do you need – IT, secretarial, admin, etc?

- If you could change three unproductive things that aren't working for you, what would they be?

- Are you being busy or productive? How can you streamline your business and free up more time?

- Consider passive income. How can you make money without being present?

- What could seriously and dramatically improve your working day?

Be warned – running on empty and burnout are common side-effects of running your own business. It is 100 percent your own responsibility to take care of your health and well-being to ensure you are at your best at all times. Having your own business should be about having greater freedom and choice and not about being chained to your desk and working around the clock. Put yourself on the top of your care list each day and the rest will follow.

CHAPTER 6

Market research:
Know your client

"I was 16 when I first started, with no qualifications, no money, just a dream in my head, and I made every mistake in the book, and now I've started all over again. And I've made every mistake in the book. [Even with] age and experience, you still need to make mistakes. I always think that failure is the doorstep to success."

Jo Malone
The Apprentice, BBC One,
3 June 2012

> *I like being my own boss. I don't respond well to authority and routine. I get bored very easily!*

Sarah Hancox

S ARAH WAS born in Australia to English parents. Her father's job in computers meant that she moved back and forth between the two countries. At 17, while in London, she found work as an administrator in the City.

She needed to help pay off some debts that her boyfriend had incurred. So she began working at the *Evening Standard* during the day, and a restaurant in Putney in the evenings and at weekends. When the relationship eventually disintegrated and she left him, she discovered that she was looking forward to going to work at the restaurant – and making a lot of money in tips.

> **DREAM BUSINESS OWNER**
>
> **Sarah Hancox**
> Vite.net.au,
> Adelaide, Australia
>
> **JOURNEY**
>
> Sales ➡ Founder of corporate catering company

"I didn't want to go back to an office, so I went full-time at the restaurant. I was able to think about my own career for the first time in seven years. I was earning £150 a week and my rent was £115. But it's amazing what you can do when you're forced to. I decided to enroll in a Higher National Diploma (HND) in hospitality. It was a great course and I went on to do a top-up year and gained my BA Hons. It was fantastically resourced and the lecturers were full of enthusiasm. It taught me so much about food, but also about business – human resources management, basic accountancy, rotas, sales and marketing.

"Following the HND I got a job working as an operations manager in the City. During this time I met a lot of different and experienced people who had a great influence on me."

Armed with her new training and experience, she went into business with her brother and they bought a restaurant. But Sarah soon began to feel the strains of a seven-day operation with a late licence. She enjoyed it less and less as drinking in the UK became more "full-on and aggressive" and the business became more and more about the bar. It lasted six years.

She married, and wanted to spend more time with her husband. They decided they couldn't achieve that in the UK. A couple of holidays in Australia had made them fond of Adelaide. They saw its potential for a more laidback lifestyle. They took the plunge and moved to Oz.

"I was emotionally exhausted and in a broken-down state. I took six months out and eventually recovered and got a temping job. But the days dragged, so I went into real estate. I needed a change from the 24-hour responsibility of being self-employed. I worked in real estate for 18 months.

"Real estate in South Australia is run very much like having your own business. You provide the finance to market yourself, you arrange all your own appointments, you work on your own, and you sell the property. But the pay was commission-based and the stress of waiting for cash to come in made me realise that I might as well be genuinely self-employed again."

Researching the market

"While in real estate I had started thinking about the food business again and as we became more familiar with Adelaide and the market, it seemed to become a real possibility.

"I started as a small stall in a food court within a shopping mall. I cooked in the morning and served the food, and it was all gone by lunchtime. It enabled me to have a really good look at how Adelaide worked, how it dressed, how much money people had. It was a great insight into the market. Without realising I was doing it, I was looking in the Businesses For Sale section in the paper and came across a very cheap food outlet in the city centre.

"We were sitting in the back garden one hot summer night, drinking a great bottle of South Australian wine, lamenting the fact that it was very hard to buy something other than Asian fast food for lunch in the city centre. I already knew what type of dishes people liked to buy from my experience in the restaurant and wondered if I could produce that type of food for the price that people were prepared to pay for lunch. My husband works in marketing and I have always been a believer in strong marketing. By the time we finished the bottle, we had a framework – the name, how the shopfront would look, the menu and what equipment would be needed, who the customers would be and how to reach them."

Researching the food court

"I sat every day for a week just watching what went on in the food court – when it was busy, who was purchasing, what they were purchasing, what they looked like, who was just walking through, where else they shopped.

"I then approached my bank. Having an appropriate qualification and lots of experience is always a good thing when talking to banks. And they definitely will want to see a business plan. Put everything into it – it doesn't matter how trivial it may be.

"I spoke to all of my friends and associates who buy their lunch in the city and I ate at a lot of different outlets to see what the quality and pricing was like.

"I did approach a local business enterprise council but for some reason they were very unhelpful and told me that there wasn't a market for what I wanted to do. True to my character, I ignored everything they said and pushed it to the back of my mind.

"I was offered a business loan and credit card by the bank. We did a soft opening and just let the clientele slowly increase over the first week, before launching into any advertising.

"I like being my own boss. I don't respond well to authority and routine. I get bored very easily! My business has moved, from a food court stall to a café, then to catering for a conference centre, and now to catering for a corporate market. South Australia is very much a Monday-to-Friday society. I saw an opportunity to do what I love and still have weekends with my husband."

Sarah's mentor

"I did have a mentor, although I didn't realise it until years later: my boss, when I was an operations manager. He was an accountant with a food background. He always faced difficult situations with humour, but he also taught me the importance of budget control when you're dealing with food. He often made decisions that would confuse and frustrate me. But now, years later, I find myself doing and saying the things he did and said.

Sarah's biggest challenge

"Managing cash flow, and being undercapitalised – you can never have enough capital to start with and there will always be bills popping up that you didn't account for."

Sarah's biggest success

"This year, and just recently, it was being able to tender for catering contracts and get them. Last year – hitting my target for food cost, labour cost and turnover, all together in the same month! In the previous business – my restaurant in Hitchin was reviewed as one of Britain's most authentic restaurants. I wasn't even in the country! I was very proud of my staff, who maintained their high standards and customer service when the boss wasn't around.

"And above everything else, seeing my staff happy at work and enjoying their own successes."

What would Sarah have done differently?

"Have more money to start off with! And make sure to always have some capital in the bank.

"In the early days I should have tried not to do everything myself and to delegate a bit more. Try to relax and enjoy the process."

Sarah's inspirations

"I like Veuve Clicquot – besides being a yummy champagne, they have a consistent, international brand that inspires people to buy. Yet when you go to Champagne the grapes used are grown and farmed by many small families, still using traditional methods."

Sarah's attitude to the recession

"Yes, people are not spending as much. However, there is less competition because catering businesses close. You simply have to focus on things like customer service, value and quality."

Sarah's attitude to social networking

"It isn't necessary. For me it's all about personal contact and attention. I have friends who have their own businesses and they just seem to spend all their time updating, reading, freaking out about negative responses, and not doing what they do best – which is running their business. I join networking forums and make business contacts that way. People remember you, and your reputation spreads through word of mouth. Once you work for a client and do a good job, they don't go elsewhere."

Sarah's Secrets

TO DREAM BUSINESS SUCCESS

"

1 Know your industry, take time to learn your trade.

2 Be honest with yourself about what your customers want. Watch what they do – not what they say!

3 Be prepared for a 24/7 commitment.

4 Continue to actively market your business, especially in the downtime.

5 Understand that you are only as good as your staff and that they are your biggest asset.

6 Go out of your way for your customers.

"

COACHING TIPS #6

Goals + Vision = Success

Goals are like the stepping stones that will take you to your vision. We need short-, medium- and long-term goals to move us along, to have something to aspire to and to act as landmarks in our business success. You might want to think about a monthly goal, a goal for three months' time and one for a year from now.

Your goals may change as your business evolves and that's OK too. The main thing is to get clarity as to what it is you're aiming for.

Typical business goals include:

- Turnover for the business

- Customer/client numbers

- Client retention

- Costs of running the business

- Repeat orders

- Profitability

- Personal drawing from the business – how many business owners forget to draw a salary?

- Placement in marketplace

- Reputation and brand awareness

- Possibility of expansion

Don't forget to think about personal goals, too. It is important to remember all aspects of your life, not just your business in isolation, in order to have the perfect work-life balance. After all, there would be no victory and joy in creating a successful business if it came at an irretrievable cost to your family, relationships or health.

Typical personal goals might include:

- Starting a new and absorbing hobby

- Having time to exercise, play sports, keep fit

- Enjoying quality time with family and friends

- Going for regular salon treatments

- Taking more mini holidays or weekend breaks

- Making financial investments, such as in property or stocks

- Looking good and dressing well

- Eating healthy organic foods and drinking lots of water

- Giving up toxic habits – smoking, drinking alcohol to excess, too much coffee, fast foods, etc

- Getting more sleep

Get SMART with your business and personal goals

A goal should be:
    Specific
    Measurable
    Attainable
    Realistic
    Timely

Write down your goals and put them some place you can see them regularly. Imagine the thrill as you reach your goal and then set another even more exciting one. Use your goals to keep you motivated and inspired.

Creative competition

If the thought of competition has you thinking back to the horrors of the school sports day, knees knocking in your gym shorts and heart pounding as all the leaner, meaner, faster kids flexed their muscles next to you at the starting line, then relax.

Everyone needs competition. It keeps us sharp and gives us an edge that can help define our businesses. Accept the fact that competition will never go away. It's as much a part of your success as your client base.

There is no point adopting an ostrich approach to competition. It won't serve you to ignore what other people are doing. Regularly review the competition so you can 'up' your offer, check the market value of your service, get new ideas, create further niches and update your message.

If you are feeling threatened by your competitors, you are coming from a point of neediness, and fear is never an attractive message to send out to your clients or customers. Try instead to come from a position of abundance – there is plenty to go around, provided you are secure in what you do and the unique services you offer.

Competition never goes away, no matter how much you may wish it. There will always be a new kid on the block offering something different. Your success depends on how you roll with the changes and move with the tide. Don't ignore fashion changes or badmouth them to clients and customers – it will all backfire on you.

Competition as allies

The danger with competition is to obsess so much about it that you get bogged down with what others are doing while not paying attention to your own business. Keep competition in perspective. In fact, why not go a step further and embrace your competitors?

Strategic Alliance Partnerships (SAPs) could help you increase your business and develop further niches. Go and meet people who do what you do and find out how they do business, create support and referral groups, discuss how you work differently and see how you can dovetail your services.

Why not offer to share website addresses on your websites or refer other people in your profession if you are unable to handle the business?

For example, coaches could form SAPs with other coaches, psychotherapists, hypnotherapists, personal trainers, beauty salons, gyms, counsellors, business groups, alternative healers, schools, women's groups, etc.

What SAPs could *you* create? Don't be afraid to go and see your main competitor. Perhaps you could support each other in more ways than you think.

CHAPTER 7

Rise of the *She*-conomy

"A woman is like a tea bag; you never know how strong it is until it's in hot water."

Eleanor Roosevelt

'Can we talk to the boss?' 'You're talking to the boss.' 'No, really, can we talk to the boss?'

Michelle Brown

MICHELLE HAS HAD her own public relations business for 24 years and is one of the most well-connected people in the PR industry in South Africa.

She is now highly regarded locally as the 'go to' person for hosting, running and co-ordinating functions, guest appearances, fund-raisers, market days, book launches. In 2010 she was asked to work for FIFA during the World Cup.

DREAM BUSINESS OWNER

Michelle Brown
Founder and owner,
Browns PR,
South Africa

JOURNEY

Corporate employee ➜
Sole trader

"South Africa is an entrepreneurial country. We had sanctions against us up to 1994 and that forced us to start our own businesses rather than rely on corporates, who were withdrawing from the country. And now, the unemployment produced by the global recession is forcing people to look to see how they can start their own businesses.

"One of the events we are running is a Market Day for a national television station for 400 kids aged between 7 and 15. They submit an entry form with a business plan. It's training them to be business moguls. One girl from a farming area set up a cutlery business and I use her at my events. She was 12 when she started with me. From a little farm and she made hand-painted cutlery. She won Best Stall. At 16 she's now employing three women from a local rural area. She exports and has orders from shops in and around South Africa."

Michelle's own entrepreneurial career started while she was doing PR for a corporate company.

"My boss called me in and said, 'People are always phoning you for advice and asking you how to organise this, where to get that from, who to contact here – why don't you set up your own events company?' I've always organised things and I've always been involved with people. I think I can safely say I've always been regarded as a leader, at school and in my community. So, I followed his advice and I started Browns PR, in my dining room. Twenty-four years later I'm still in an office in my home – it's me and my mornings-only PA."

Starting out

Michelle started her business when her little boy was 3. "Like all entrepreneurs and business owners, I was excited, and incredibly scared. But, you know, scared is good.

"I just knew I could do it. I had built up a solid reputation in Port Elizabeth with corporate clients and always delivered what was promised. I had worked hard to do that. I considered myself professional and so I think that pulls you through. Your name is all you have in the beginning. When I talk to students I get them to understand that no one can take your name away, but they can take your reputation from you. So you have to conduct yourself professionally at all times. That has seen me through. Many of my corporate bosses from before I set up on my own 24 years ago are still my clients today.

"People think it's easy. They see the glamorous side of my industry, they see you at functions and events, they see you with celebrities, but they don't see what goes on seven weeks before then. They don't see the long hours, the weekends at work. So there's a misconception that the industry is easy.

"I don't think people do their homework properly. People take things for granted. You're not going to get work on a plate. Previously, you knew someone or your parents knew someone – that doesn't happen anymore. It's a tough world out there."

Michelle's biggest challenge

"As a woman, to be taken seriously. And it still is. I'm 55 years old and, after 20 years in the business, I still get the attitude, 'Can we talk to your boss?' 'You're talking to the boss.' 'No really, can we talk to the boss?'

"I know it's the 21st century, but women still have to work very hard to be taken seriously in the world of business. In spite of corporates saying we've got 47 percent women on our board, when the tea tray comes into the boardroom meeting... It happened to me when I was attending a meeting in Johannesburg. They put the tea tray down in the centre of the table. Everyone looked at me and I thought, 'I'm not pouring the tea just because I'm the only woman in the room!' So I looked at my diary and pretended to be very busy until the CEO of the company said, 'Mrs Brown, would you like a cup of tea?' I said, 'Yes, I thought you'd never ask.'"

Michelle's biggest success

"The 2010 World Cup in South Africa, when FIFA appointed me the venue media officer at the Nelson Mandela Stadium. That for me was a 'Yes! You do have what it takes to do this.' They emailed me and I cried. I phoned my husband, phoned my kids, phoned my brothers. I was incredibly proud to represent my country."

What would Michelle have done differently?

"Nothing. I'm really happy as to how it's panned out. I've worked so hard and I'm proud of working hard. Holding my head up high as a woman in business. My late mum and my late dad gave me a very good grounding. But at the end of the day, South Africa World Cup or not, my kids come first. Always."

Michelle's attitude to the recession

"The corporates are having smaller events and not having as many as they used to. But that forces me to think out of the box. It forces me to concentrate on other aspects of PR and to up my game. Without that, you can find yourself resting on your laurels a little bit."

Michelle's attitude to social networking

"I think it's very important. But there is nothing that beats face-to-face communication."

What does Michelle wish she'd known before she started out?

"I knew it would be hard, because I've always worked since I was very young. But I always worked in a corporate infrastructure, so I wish I'd known how hard 'hard' really was. You have to thrive on challenges. It's been proven to me time and again that things happen for a reason. If you don't get a job that you've pitched for, it's because there's something else on the horizon."

Michelle's Secrets
TO DREAM BUSINESS SUCCESS

1 Always deliver on what you promise; if you slip up just once, that's what people will remember.

2 You've got to start at the bottom and work your way up, you've got to work after hours, you've got to work weekends – that's just the name of the game.

3 Under-promise and over-deliver.

Continued overleaf

"

4 There are only 24 hours in a day. The thing that separates you from the competition is how you utilise those hours. Time management and organisation skills are imperative whatever industry you are in. I'll fetch the laundry in between meetings. And I'll buy supper in between meetings. Because all that's got to fit into my day.

5 Network and follow up. If you give me your business card, I will follow up with an email about how good it was to meet you and look forward to getting together. And if I ever see or read something about you in the press or on social media I will email and say how fabulous to see your article in the paper. I saw that your son has just been made a Springbok rugby player, congratulations. That's also being media-aware.

6 Do your homework. Do your research. Find out who else is running the same kind of business. What are they good at and what can you do to be better or to up your game? Is there a market for what you want to do? If there are 20 other businesses in your city doing exactly the same thing, unless you up your game or do it slightly differently, you are not going to do well or be successful.

7 Have your wits about you. Have a good network that can back you up and support you, because you can't be good at everything or know everything.

"

COACHING TIPS #7

Hold the front page!
Getting featured in the press

When you have a super-charged business, when it's up and running and the feedback has been good, then it's time to go up a level and tell a wider audience about where you are and what you do. This is when you might like to consider getting some press coverage.

The benefits of getting featured in a newspaper or magazine are manifold. You will raise your profile and gain credibility, extend your competitive edge, get broadcast to a wider audience and yes, get more clients and sales. Publishers and television producers, too, are much more interested in you if you have a proven track record of being newsworthy.

And probably the best thing of all is that press coverage is free. This is an important point – you don't have to pay to get coverage. If you do that is called advertising or an advertorial. There is a difference.

Even if you feel what you are doing isn't so original, you need to define an angle about you or your business which could be of interest to the press.

What's your line

When thinking up a good story you need to be creative. The journalist doesn't want to think about how they can use you on their precious pages so make it easy for them by coming up with great ideas.

When defining what line you could create about your business consider these possible directions:

- Using you and your story as a case-study – "I changed my life by leaving the nursing service to become a horse whisperer"

- Using your clients as stories – "X helped me lose seven stone and rediscover my inner diva"

- Before-and-after makeovers with clients' photos and testimonials

- How you and your services or products are different from the rest – a well-honed USP is needed here

- Seasonal campaigns – "Detox your house/life/lover/pet for Christmas with our amazing gizmo"

- Find stats, facts and figures to get attention – "20 million people will be thinking about investing in starfish this season"

Placing the story

Now it's time to do your research. Where will your story go? Is it a women's interest story – if so, what age group? Who is your demographic – elite, family, high-end, inclusive, exclusive, creative, middle of the road?

Start to familiarise yourself with publications that you want to target. Who edits the pages your story would go on? Often there is a directory at the beginning of a glossy magazine listing who the features teams are. You can phone the switchboard or look online for the reporter who covers the stories most suited to your theme.

A good place to start is your local press, who will want feel-good stories from people who live and work in the area. This could be the start of your cuttings file.

Your press starter kit

Before you even consider contacting a magazine or paper, make sure you have the following:

- A professionally taken colour photograph of you and your products

- A mini bio about you and your business (not too long)

- A punchy press release outlining your story

- A list of ten top tips on a subject relating to what you do, e.g. "Ten things you didn't know about eyebrow shaping" or "Ten ways to pack for the perfect ski holiday." These tips are also great as free downloads on your website or for handing out at networking meetings.

- Don't forget your contact details, availability for interview, client case-studies, etc

The Do's and Don'ts of talking to the press

If emailing a journalist be sure to put in the subject line, "A feature idea for your fashion/food/lifestyle/new buys pages," and then put your press release below and attach your bio and photos. You can also phone a journalist and offer to pay a visit or invite them to your launch or to sample your products or services.

Don't

- Don't inundate the journalist with information, facts and figures unless they ask for it.

- Don't expect to see the copy before it goes to print. Don't ask to see it either – it annoys them.

- Don't expect to be told when it will be published – the writer may not even know.

- Don't expect that your story is guaranteed to appear. Journalists interview a lot of people; don't be offended if your quote wasn't used. It's not personal.

- Don't expect to be sent a copy of the publication. You have to buy your own.

Do

- Learn to give quotes in good soundbites; don't waffle.

- Thank the journalist after it has gone in.

- Use the piece when it comes out – on your website and pro-motional literature, e.g. "As seen in *Homes and Gardens*" or "As featured in *The Times*."

- Add the piece to your blog and tweet it.

- Keep in touch with the writer, not immediately after, but in the future and with another idea.

- Think of other publications who might want something simi-lar and recycle the idea.

It takes tenacity, it's not guaranteed and it can take some time, but getting press coverage can seriously enhance your business success. Journalists need your stories to fill their pages.

Why not be the Next Big Thing?

CHAPTER 8

Riders of the storm:
How to rise after the falls

" In the UK 45.7 percent of those asked cited 'fear of failure' as the reason preventing them from setting up their own business. "

Global Entrepreneurship Monitor UK
2011 Monitoring Report

66 *The world has many great companies and many great products. You have the potential to be brilliant. But some never quite get out there for people to know who they are. What you have to do is get known, somehow.* 99

David Peto

DAVID RAN a tech company in Soho with some friends and devoted much of his life to it. But then it went wrong. David's story is a great one to show how you can rebuild yourself from rock bottom, recover and create something superior.

He started out in life hoping to be an actor, but instead became a successful entrepreneur. "I had no clear path to get to here. From the time I was small I wanted to be an actor. I was the short, non-sporty, slightly fat kid in school. But when I walked out on stage suddenly everyone paid attention. That sticks. So all the way through school I was in plays, learning how to film, learning how to edit.

DREAM BUSINESS OWNER

David Peto
Founder and CEO, Aframe, UK

JOURNEY

Freelance actor ➡ Tech entrepreneur

"Everybody else had a gap year, but I wanted to *do* something. I was a geek and I worked with computers since I was tiny. I loved technology so I applied for a pre-university placement at IBM. If you like technology IBM is an incredible place. It's where I got my first taste of business. I was 18 and ended up running a department with a million-pound budget – which was nuts!"

Following his IBM placement, David got offered a few jobs but still wanted to be an actor. He went to university as his parents were keen he had a backup in case things didn't work out. "I went to Warwick to do a degree and whilst there also acted and made films."

Pursuing his dream David then went to drama school in London. He secured an agent and started acting.

"I occasionally got paid and did a few bad TV adverts. But I kept turning up on set and realised that people didn't know how to make it. People had no idea about budgeting or how to organise the production process. It was a mess, so I started getting asked to go behind the camera and help. As pointed out by my girl-friend, I very quickly got offered more money doing that than I did acting. I did sound design, acting, I produced plays, films. It's not what you'd expect for someone who goes on to be CEO of a tech company."

During that time David met an old school friend who, by coinci-dence, had a production company, and he joined forces with them to help on the business side.

"I joined him as their producer. While running that company, we built a system that would do high-definition video editing at a really, really low cost. The phone was ringing off the hook with people wanting to use it. And that's what sparked the idea of starting up the post-production company."

The start-up process

"We didn't have much of a clue, but having a business plan and being 26 in 2006 was enough to get a loan. We raised half a million pounds and with all the wonderful naivety in the world started the first ever digital post-production company in Soho, London. And we started taking all the work from people who had been doing it more expensively for ages."

David and his partners, Tom (COO and creative producer) and Roland (special effects extraordinaire), came in and did it differently. They were digital and therefore faster, more efficient. They provided excellent customer service, which enabled them to compete with the other companies, who'd been around for years doing it their way.

"We had £3.5 million worth of turnover and we did that from scratch. We were basically the scourge of the industry ('We've been doing this for 30 years – who are these kids?'). And there were terrible times and great times. There were times we were looking at the bank balance and thinking, 'How the hell are we going to pay anybody?' But because people believed in what we were doing, it was a terrific thing.

"We did the same great quality of work, if not better, but crucially we were considerably cheaper. Plus we were really approachable. We couldn't afford to rest on our laurels. And our ethos was about being friendly and doing good work. That's what people always loved about the company."

PR

"I was cold calling and saying, 'I hear you've got a final cut – this is what we do.' But we hired someone in who had better relationships than us. The advantage of our industry is that it's big but it's also small. People talk and if you do a good job – then word spreads quite quickly. We did a lot of the PR. We had a good story as we were three young people starting out. So we used press coverage. At any drinks event I was the last to leave.

"We did a small job for £70. Then we'd get another job for £100. Then we'd get bigger jobs for £2000–6000. All because we'd done that first job at £70 and they'd liked it. By the end of it we were doing £250,000 jobs without thinking about it. People ask, 'How do I get that quarter-of-a-million-pound job?' My advice would be, do the £70 job first, do it well and see what follows. We had no reputation, and people didn't know if we were any good – so we had to just get people to come in and give them a go on something. If we had let them down it wouldn't matter, but if it went well and it was a great price then people started to talk about it."

Like any new company, David's needed to be known – so he networked. He built relationships and trust, which created a strong foundation for the company.

"We started with six edit suites and there were six of us running this thing. We were all working crazy hours. I was up in the morning at 6 am working through to 7.30 pm, then entertaining clients. I was desperately trying to get new people till two in the morning – and then doing it again the next day, ad infinitum. One day as I was walking up the stairs to my flat, blood came pouring out of my nose and it wouldn't stop. I was whisked off to hospital where they found a vein had burst in my head. They told me it was caused by stress and I couldn't go back to work for a few weeks. I was back in two days. We took it from six staff and six suites, to 50 staff and 22 edit suites and a big visual effects department, and we did all of Sky HD's adverts."

Baby steps

"People turn round and say, 'Wow, look what you've done' and all this rubbish, but every single bit – it's just baby steps. If you look at anyone who's got ten million dollars or 100 million dollars of turnover, you're never going to do it because it seems impossible. But you just start. You pick up the phone to one person and say, 'Hello, how about this?' It's little steps and suddenly you realise you've made big progress without noticing it. You get momentum behind you because people see it and they start to offer more help and then it starts to snowball. But it's just those first few steps at the beginning you have to take."

Complications

David and the team raised more finance and were about to open in New York but they had made a key mistake. "We chose the wrong investor, who just wasn't the right fit for the company. Externally the business was a resounding success but internally we were all unhappy." David resigned. His partners followed shortly afterwards and set up another company.

"You have to realise when you're unhappy. It's very hard sometimes. You get so inured to a certain level of pain it's very hard to lift your head back and say, "This isn't right, I'm unhappy." I had a mortgage and monthly bills but I walked out of the building and it was very sad. I'd built up this whole company, it felt like it was me. Your ego is so tied to it. I felt like a film star who'd failed. I walked home and sat down and this weight just lifted and you just know at that point that it wasn't right anyway."

When David left the company he describes himself as a "wreck." He had poured all his passion and energy into the company and it was very difficult to leave it behind and move on.

"I went quiet. I didn't want people asking me what I wanted to do next – I'd created this one company, was I going to manage to do it again? Also, I had ground myself down so badly. I was drinking more and not doing any exercise. I was very lethargic and didn't do anything other than get through the day."

Recovery

"I spent time with friends, rather than business colleagues, and just regrounded myself in thinking about what to do next. My girlfriend did ask if I didn't just want to get a proper job! But I couldn't do that – I've never really worked for anyone else. When you're low it's really important to make space and I took time to reflect on my strengths and weaknesses. I just made lists and was brutally honest. I am good at finding people, getting teams together. Bad at detail and making sure payments are made on time. I also looked at the causes of my shying away from doing certain things. Did I have money issues? What people thought of me was very important – why was that?

"You get your drive in many different ways. When I was at school I was never exactly the popular kid. And so a lot of the drive comes from what you want to show people. So I think I've gone from that – the person no one pays any attention to – to now doing this kind of a thing. But also I love waking up in the morning and not knowing what is going to happen. The worst nightmare for me ever would be waking up and knowing that the next ten weeks were going to be exactly the same. If this new company did do really well and we sold out and I made a lot of money, would I go and lie on a beach? That would drive me insane. And I think even if a day's awful, it's still a different day."

To maintain his stamina David runs and goes to the gym. "Most of my business ideas come up when I'm on really, really long runs. At the moment, though, every single minute I'm not doing this I'm with my baby daughter."

Starting again

David sat down with his accountant and set about creating a new company. He wrote down the big idea. It began as a three-page document, but grew to five. He then did his research by getting on the train to meet the experts in his chosen field.

Which experts? "This guy's big in the world of metadata – let's go and meet him. This person knows all about technical storage – let's go and meet him. Choose someone you know you'll never want to do business with – pick up the phone and ask him all the really stupid questions. He'll think you're an idiot but it doesn't matter. I always phrase it with, 'I'd love to come and ask your advice.' People seem to love that. Use what you learn from them and talk to the second person. You'll sound a little bit less like an idiot. Then you phone the person you really want to speak to and you sound like you really know what you're talking about.

"I sat down and wrote a list of all the people who might invest. I contacted someone who would have invested in our New York expansion. I rang someone who'd been introduced to me as a potential investor and took him for lunch to tell him this is what I'm doing, this is where it is. And he said, 'Fine – I'll give you ten grand.'"

Terrifying

David makes it all sound very straightforward. But, just like anyone else, when he makes these calls he's really scared. "It's terrifying. Nobody likes rejection. The only advantage I have is I've been an actor – I've been through hundreds of auditions and been rejected countless times. But I'm still terrified now that they'll say no. I want to talk to the head of digital strategy at ITV – never met them. They might not even like the idea of Aframe. But you've still got to try and get hold of them. It's not easy."

Whilst David was raising money for his new company idea, he didn't tell anybody about it in the industry. Everybody was made to sign non-disclosure agreements.

"I was worried about people doing something similar before we did and I was really enjoying building it all and there was no one to impress except me. I also wanted to be able to come out with something that worked. Once I'd delivered on what I said I was going to, it was easier when I came to raising the next £300k, which ended up being £500k. The investors all went out to their friends saying, 'Here's David, he's already done this.' Which helped me raise that next round of money."

David then moved into offices and brought in the first team of developers.

"Again I didn't tell anybody. I just kept building and putting it to the test. I brought in clients to try it. Some of them were old clients and some were new ones who just loved the idea and wanted to give it a go. We still have our first invoice framed. A lot of people will buy into the future of what you're doing. They understand that it's not perfect yet, and that it still has problems. But they also know you're going to look after them and love them so much, just as long as you don't let them down you price it accordingly. It's not as hard as you may think to find people who'll buy into that. Find someone to be your first case-study. Give them a great price in exchange for a case-study. We contacted Ten Alps (Bob Geldof's production company) – they used us on a project with Richard Dawkins."

Aframe is a way of storing and working with video from anywhere and is different to the public clouds already available. "Video requires a huge file size and people want to work all over the place. The clouds out there aren't designed for that. We specialise in video so ours is tailored to that which gives us a lot of performance gains and works better for us cost-wise. The public clouds are expensive.

"All we ever projected was that we cared about your project. We wanted people to know that nothing is more important to us than the safety and security of their video content. So we don't trust anybody else to do it for us – we do it ourselves. And once we started to get that message out it's a big reason we have won some of the customers we have. People realise we have the technical expertise to do it ourselves but more importantly you're buying into a company that cares about what you do."

David's biggest challenge

"Raising this last round of money in this market was unbelievably hard. So many times we were nearly there and then it didn't happen and we had to start from scratch. I have done over 100 pitches. We had to get the money in order to grow – and get huge – so this last round was $7 million. I can now sleep at night because we have that money in the bank. I raised the smaller sums first and built up from there. It's all about the little steps that get you to those kinds of places."

David's biggest success

"Seeing the people who work for me in the past go on to do the most amazing things. I'm proud of the businesses I've set up but I'm also proud about the people I've given a chance to. A business is just a business – it's nothing without the people.

"The jobs we've created in the North East of England – the people there are amazing, the most loyal I've ever met. They're all local because there are a lot of very talented people who can't get a job."

David's Secrets
TO DREAM BUSINESS SUCCESS

"

1 It's OK to make mistakes. It doesn't mean everyone thinks you're an idiot or that everyone is going to lose faith in you. If you look at a lot of companies from the outside they seem glossy and perfect, and you think, 'How am I going to ever be as good as that?' But you soon discover that internally everyone is the same – everyone is making mistakes. And learning.

2 Never be afraid to ask for help.

3 Always employ people better than you. You need people to challenge you, give you advice and tell you you're wrong. I also hire people who do all the bits I'm bad at.

4 You need to have a business plan. And work out what your strengths and weaknesses are.

5 Go and meet as many people as you can. Before you set up your website or anything else, just go out and learn.

6 I love my sleep. If you have sleep problems you'll burn yourself out.

Continued overleaf

> 66
>
> **7** I hate Dragons' Den and The Apprentice. They breed this cult of The Entrepreneur, but an entrepreneur is nothing more than a business person who is able to come up with ideas. You can have the greatest idea but if you cannot deliver, you'll never get anywhere.
>
> 99

What would David have done differently?

"At Aframe I was very worried about people stealing the idea or being negative about it. But once we went public, all sorts of people popped out of the woodwork to help. Had I done that a year early I might have got further along the line quicker."

David's attitude to the recession

"I've only ever had a business in a recession. The number of great businesses starting in a recession is disproportionately high – Google and Amazon, for example. It's because people get made redundant so they take the opportunity to start their businesses. But also, business customers tend to change their practices only if they're in pain. Why swap from the supplier you've had for 50 years? Why use these guys who may be way more efficient but whom you don't know? You do it because you have to."

David's inspirations

"Marc Benioff, founder of Sales Force, took on the giants of the industry much as we are doing, with a lot less money, and has been so successful that his major competitors have either gone bust or got bored. In the beginning, at the big conferences he couldn't afford a stand, so he hired a big band outside, waving banners saying, 'Don't go in there, buy our product!' He would prebook all the taxis at the airport so people going to the conference had to be talked to by his staff in the taxi. I love these irreverent manoeuvres."

Anything David wishes he'd known before starting out?

"No. If you knew what you had to do to get to where you are, you'd never do it."

> **Success for me is how many people you touch positively, how many people you do something for.**

Diana Verde Nieto II

DIANA WAS born and educated in Buenos Aires. Her childhood was not easy. Brought up under a brutal dictatorship until she was 10, she vividly remembers the day the army came to a neighbour's house and took away the parents of her school friend.

At university, life seemed to be going well for Diana when she met and fell in love with an English boy, whom she dated for two years before coming to the UK to be with him. "I arrived with a hard-earned $500 in my suitcase. But he wasn't at the airport to meet me – he was in Prague, with his girlfriend of five years. I went over to Prague, but it was a disastrous trip. I rang my dad and said, 'I'm coming home.' He said, 'Stay.'"

DREAM BUSINESS OWNER

Diana Verde Nieto II
Founder and CEO,
positiveluxury.com

JOURNEY

Dog-walker ➡
Social entrepreneur and
World Economic Forum
Young Global Leader

So she stayed. And things began to look up. "My boyfriend's friend took pity on me and said I could stay at his house." She went on to marry him, and they were together for 13 years.

Diana found adjusting to the UK difficult. It was October and the weather was awful. "I stayed in for two months. He said, 'Why don't you go out?' I said, 'I'm waiting for the rain to stop.' Because that's what we do at home. I didn't realise that in the UK it rains all the time!" She had endless waitressing and bar jobs. "I even got fired from walking dogs because I let the dogs off their leads."

And then she had a breakthrough. At home in Argentina, she had grown up listening to the World Service and had set her sights on working at the BBC.

"I saw a job advert in *The Guardian* and I said, 'That's my job!' I got called for an interview, but only because the interviewer had been impressed with my sports record. Still, I phoned him every day. Sheer persistence got me the job. I worked hard to learn English. And I really loved it."

She worked for BBC Worldwide licensing radio programmes to Latin America and – as the internet began to really take off – started working on the corporation's online strategy. "There was a huge appetite in Latin America for British broadcasting and you could see how the internet could become this global way of sharing content."

She moved to an Internet Service Provider, developing content, then to Scoot.com, working in business development. "It was a fast-paced environment and there was a high turnover of jobs. In a month you could be a CEO. I learnt a huge amount – we were talking about online and mobile payments before PayPal and talking about voice recognition before Google." A victim of the dot-com crash, Scoot folded and Diana decided to rethink everything. She took time off, flew to Australia and went diving on the Great Barrier Reef.

A pivotal moment

It turned out to be a pivotal moment in Diana's career.

"I was diving near Fraser Island, hoping to see coral, but they were all dead – you could only see lionfish. Back on land I met this guy in a bar who turned out to be a marine biologist and we started talking about what had happened. He explained how climate change was devastating the delicate Barrier Reef ecosystem. All this beauty was disappearing right in front of my eyes."

Back home her husband was going through a career change, switching from advertising to studying environmental technology at Imperial College.

"I was putting all of this together with ideas about my upbringing under a regime that ignored human rights. Sustainability was not something people really cared about so I was trying to work out how to spread the word. I knew business had to be part of the solution rather than only seen as the enemy so I decided to launch a business myself – a communications consultancy, something that would help businesses change and work to raise awareness of threats to the environment. My husband said, 'Why don't you get a job?' He told me I was crazy but we agreed that if in six months I had earned no money, I would have to go out to work."

Trying to come up with a name, she was looking through a book on the Great Barrier Reef and reading about the amazing symbiosis of the rich reef life – especially the clownfish and its anemone host (this was before Finding Nemo). "So I called the company Clownfish for luck. I started by pitching to every brand and every journalist I could find, thinking this was marketing and media, but it turned out that – at that time in the UK – sustainability was looked after by the health and safety department!"

She found more fertile ground in Europe and pitched for trend-forecasting work from the mobile arms of German electronics giant Siemens. "We talked about long-term trends, about how we could get terms like 'green' and 'sustainable development' into the mainstream, and we won it. They became our first client."

Accepted business wisdom has it that the first three years of any start-up are the hardest. "They were tough times – the economy was contracting, but we were growing, taking every job we could."

The big chance

Then she heard that Al Gore was filming his breakthrough movie An Inconvenient Truth and looking for companies to help promote the film in an unconventional way: persuading leading Fortune 500 companies to screen the movie to their employees, alerting them to its message.

It was Diana's big chance and she took the plunge. Clownfish had no experience in the film industry so she was outside her comfort zone, but she believed in the project so passionately the NGO took her on. The key, she believes, was that she didn't pretend to have the experience – but she knew she had the skills to deliver.

"We did a good job, and of course we built some very good contacts in Fortune 500 companies," she laughs. "I'd been nervous pitching for that business – we'd never had a piece of work that size before so I *was* scared, though not of failing. I was more scared of going back home to tell my father that I'd failed. Failure itself is intrinsic to success. You have to fail in order to get somewhere. It's like running a marathon. You can't run a marathon tomorrow but you can train for a marathon. To train you have to run every day. You feel your body being conditioned and every time you push a little bit more. Then you cross the line and look back and think, 'Wow, I did that.' You feel exhausted and you throw up and you can't walk for a week, but then you can't wait for the next one! It's like a drug."

"Running the business was the same day-by-day training. Something happens and you go with it to the next stage. I thought about building and growing – I didn't think about an exit strategy. As far as I was concerned, this was what I was doing for the rest of my life. In fact, I was working my butt off – it was literally all I was doing with my life…"

Sell off

Cut to 2008. Diana was at a conference in London and fell into conversation with the head of Aegis Media. "We began to talk about working together, and continued talking after the conference was over – but always about partnership. I had no plans to sell. Then, one day, they said they wanted to buy my business. It was amazing. I asked them what that meant I would do for them – they said build this company. It felt like everyone would be happy. So I said yes, because I wanted to grow. Aegis had the biggest digital network in the world – called Isobar – and I believed digital was the way to scale the business. So we sat down and worked out the value."

She felt that getting the word out meant reaching as many people as possible and that Clownfish was still too small to have that reach.

"People talk about recycling, organic, fair trade, but people in the street can't really internalise the complexity of the issue, because it's social, environmental, and economic all at the same time. That's difficult. People can't get it, and, after all, it's not the job of the consumer to get it.

"But my vision was to scale that information and get it to the consumer. I worked in China, America, Italy and Spain. The issues are so massive around the world we are crazy to think that it is not going to affect us here in Britain. Whatever happens anywhere else, we are so connected. Companies have to internalise this, and long-term investment will have to happen. But it still hasn't happened. It's only when consumers vote with their dollars that it's going to force companies to start thinking they have to go a certain way."

Her new working schedule was brutal. She was always on aeroplanes or checking in to hotels and her personal life suffered. She lost touch with close friends and her marriage fell apart. She had sold Clownfish two days before the massive financial crash of 2008, and after two years of helping to integrate it with Aegis Media, she stepped down as CEO.

Totally lost

Despite leaving to have more free time, Diana felt empty – ironically because she had too much time on her hands. She'd put her heart and soul into the business and now didn't know what to do with herself. She worked on setting up a business in Singapore but it came to nothing.

"It was very, very hard. When I woke up in the morning I didn't have a purpose. What was I getting out of bed for? One week I lost my car twice (I had to take a taxi to find my car – how humiliating is that?). I flooded the bath, locked my keys in the house, and kept losing my phone – it was in the fridge most of the time. People asked me what I wanted to do next but I just didn't know.

"The TEDx Talks asked me to go to Sicily to talk about sustainability and I went – but the only thing I could think about describing was failure, because that's how I felt. After all the work I'd done, I hadn't changed anything, I hadn't improved anything."

Life changing

A year earlier Diana had been nominated for the Young Global Leaders programme run by the World Economic Forum – the programme identifies under-40s who look set to make a significant contribution to improving the state of the world. She'd heard nothing since the nomination but two days before her 39th birthday someone called to tell her she'd been picked to join the 300-person elite community for a five-year term. "I thought it was a practical joke – my friend Isabelle calling me from France to tease me. But here was the WEF recognising me, just as I was leaving Clownfish!

"As part of the programme the WEF took the winners to Silicon Valley, where I met Sergey Brin, Larry Page, Sheryl Sandberg, Marissa Mayer and the guys at LinkedIn. We went to Stanford and we met all the top internet companies and met their leaders one-to-one. I was with 50 other people who'd been chosen individually. I met incredible people and there was me – no company behind me, just me.

"When I returned from that trip I knew that I was ready. I

really wanted to go back to work. Sergei, Larry, Marissa – they all started from nothing. Sheryl, the most successful self-made woman in the world, worth billions of pounds today – she was an aerobics teacher! I was inspired.

"We got invited to a party with Sean Parker (who was one of the early investors in Facebook) and the people from the Founders Fund, in this incredible house in San Francisco. I bumped into a guy who started talking about his book called *Little Bets*. 'Oh, what's it about?' 'It's about people who are really successful entrepreneurs and they find failure and they come back and start different businesses.' He gave me a manuscript of this book which wasn't even finished. I read it on the plane home and it was exactly about where I was at that moment in my life. I couldn't believe it. So I came back and I told myself, 'I'm ready. I want to do something online.'"

The process

Now that she was single, Diana threw the same energy into her dating life as she had done into her business, so the most obvious new venture, she thought, was a dating site.

"Everyone says to do what you are passionate about. Well, at that point, I was passionate about dating! So I went away to research matchmaking and after three weeks I knew everything there was to know about the subject."

She took the idea to various investors but had trouble raising money. "It's a crowded market and I had nothing really original," she shrugs ruefully. "Eventually I came to realise that my real passion was still sustainability. I thought of an online guide to sustainability, so consumers could see that this brand uses child labour, this brand is organic, and so on.

"Two years before that I had presented David Attenborough with a Lifetime Achievement Award at the Natural History Museum. He told me entire species of butterfly are extinct because they were so beautiful that collectors had killed them all. In the 1980s the Blue butterfly was extinct in the UK, and there was the most successful reintroduction of this species in the world. They brought the DNA from Sweden and the butterfly started breeding again. The British Blue is now back."

That story stayed at the back of Diana's mind. She really liked how, out of this really negative story, something very positive had happened. "I had the idea of showing the social and environmental efforts that brands are making by clicking on a blue butterfly on a website." She designed a trustmark, a Blue Butterfly logo that brands could be awarded if they had the right green credentials. She also built a website to feature the brands that had earned their Blue Butterflies so consumers could choose the best-behaved brands. Thus Positive Luxury (www.positiveluxury.com) was born.

"The little blue butterfly is the first sustainability trust mark on the internet. You can track consumer intent online. It's much clearer for brands to determine what messages to push through into the mainstream. The aim is to democratise sustainability and make it open for consumers – like the Fair Trade mark or the Rainforest Alliance, but completely interactive. After selling Clownfish, the biggest challenge was finding that thing that would get me out of bed without coffee every morning and that I would feel really passionate about. I think I've found it. I do what I love and get paid for it! But finding that sweet spot was hard.

"Success for me is not how much money you have in the bank. That's not enough recognition for what you do. I don't want to be one of the nine billion people on this planet who have taken from it. I want to be one of the few million that have done something *for* it. Yes, I want to live comfortably – but what's the point of taking it to the grave? I really want to make a difference. I haven't achieved what I want to achieve yet, but I will."

What would Diana have done differently?

"Hindsight is really easy. I would probably make the same choices because even the mistakes I made allowed me to get here. As a result I'm a lot stronger as a leader, as a person and as a spokesperson for the sustainability movement."

What does Diana wish she'd known before starting out?

"I wish I'd known more about how to manage people. First time around, I didn't know how hard it was going to be. So much time and so much pain could have been saved if I'd known how to do it. This time around I feel I'm much better equipped. You have skill sets in only one area so you risk making mistakes if you want to do everything yourself. The first piece of advice I'd give

Diana's Secrets
TO DREAM BUSINESS SUCCESS

"

1 Write a business plan. Where are you going and how are you going to get there? Have a clear set of goals – as well as some medium-term targets or KPIs – so you can always keep track of where you are along the route.

2 Find your sweet spot – because it's not easy to set it up and grow it. You need to be truly passionate because you will do it for a long time, 24 hours a day!

3 Be authentic, be who you are. Leverage your skills, your strengths. I can't sell something I don't believe in.

4 It's absolutely essential to have mentors, but there's no point in having them if you're not prepared to listen.

5 Take time to play. Create distance from the day-to-day – it creates clarity.

6 Accept failure and be flexible.

"

anyone setting up a business – get a good team around you and trust them to do those things you're not so good at. I think that makes a big difference. I've learnt to trust others to do a better job than I can do."

COACHING TIPS #8

Oh no I can't, Oh yes I can!
How to develop rhino skin

The personal development guru Dale Carnegie once said: "Develop success from failures. Discouragement and failure are two of the surest stepping stones to success."

I know, there's nothing more irritating than a Pollyanna perspective when your pride is wounded. Give yourself time to think, heal, gather strength and then move on. Patience and tenacity are as important as talent and ideas in business, and being able to ride the low tides is even more important than floating when things are good.

Developing contingency plans for you and your customers is key. Just as airlines have a process if, say, a passenger loses their luggage, so you need to think of a worst-case-scenario plan.

All of us have been through times when things didn't go as we wanted, when disappointments hurt us, and when opportunity not only failed to knock but lost our address.

But very often something even better happened in the long run. In retrospect you can see it was for a reason, you learned from it and maybe even to this day feel some relief that the path didn't deliver what you initially wanted because something altogether more wonderful came along. This can happen again.

I often meet people who have had terrible business catastrophes, like David in the story we've just read, where deals have crashed, business partners have proven less than reliable and the dream failed to materialise. Yes, it's painful and mortifying but it's seldom terminal. Remember, what happened in the past may not happen again and if you take time to learn what went wrong you won't make the mistake again.

Coaching questions

- What did you learn from the disappointment or disaster? What, if anything, is the nugget of gold?

- What do you need to do differently next time and what support can you get right now?

- What might you be assuming about future possibilities that isn't helpful?

- Refocus on what did work well; concentrate on the successes

- Managing your mindset is key and it's your choice whether it's floor or soar.

- What do you need to tell yourself to keep positive?

- What do you need right now to restore your confidence?

Choose to be a victor, not a victim of what went on. Get support from people you trust. Don't be scared to ask for help and to admit what went on.

Forgive yourself and move on. You will grow from this experience.

Never give up.

CHAPTER 9

Networking:
Finding your tribe

> **66** More than 800 million people Facebook
> their lives. **99**

Julie Meyer
Entrepreneur Country

"We were sitting in Pizza Express with three kids under five, all throwing food about, and I said, 'Could I set up a networking site like a Yahoo forum but for businesses from all over the world?'"

Penny Power

FOR 'accidental entrepreneur' Penny, life is all about connecting and building relationships. She launched the Digital Youth Academy as a way of bringing young people and their digital know-how into businesses.

"I'm accidentally in business – I feel the fraud will be uncovered eventually! I wanted to be a physiotherapist, but I failed to get on the course. So I had a gap year, worked in a pub and was a Welfare Assistant in a school. Then a headhunter advised me that I ought to be in sales, so I went and worked in a telesales role in a company. It felt very alien to me. I didn't like it or the concept of a telesales script, but I found my own way through by building relationships with people. I handed in my resignation, having been offered a place at university, but a high-up boss tried to convince me not to leave.

DREAM BUSINESS OWNER

Penny Power
Co-founder,
Ecademy, UK

JOURNEY

Sales director ➡
Mum-of-three entrepreneur

"I took on board what he said and stayed in the computer world and worked my way up from Supervisor to Manager to General

Manager and finally to Sales and Marketing Director. At 28 I had a lovely Mercedes, a company car and a house. And I'd say I was a good manager. I believe in 'servant leadership,' which is about serving to ensure others are successful. So I would get excited if there was a chance to get somebody on the ground floor of telesales and then, again, the first time they got their company car. That's what really excited me – seeing other people grow."

Children

Penny started a family. She was adamant she wanted to give up work.

"I was absolutely determined to be a stay-at-home mum, but the MD came and told me that the company who owned us wanted to sell, and he wanted to do a management buyout." She met the board of directors, who said they would not invest in the buyout unless she stayed. So, after four months, she went back to work, taking her baby with her.

"She was in my arms and I breastfed in front of the board of directors. She was a really noisy feeder. After six weeks they let me go! It left me with no alternative. I stayed at home with Hannah. And then I had Ross and TJ. I got involved in the NCT (the parenting charity), joined the PTA, went into the school and drove the teachers mad offering help. I nearly became a Chelsea-tractor-driving mother. Hannah was four-and-a-half, doing well on her books, reading well. I remember picking her up from the school gate, and one of these mothers said, 'Must dash, Jack's got French lessons.' French lessons! So I got Hannah doing the flute *and* having French lessons – she was shattered!

"Mind you, that was how I really learnt to network. When you're a child and go to school your friends are presented to you. When you get your first job your colleagues are presented to you. In the world of motherhood you have no friends and you have to learn how to network. But it was really obvious I needed to do something. Thomas, my husband, really liked me working. I think it's really hard for men. They marry a dynamic business woman and then lose that woman. He really missed that woman.

"However, I wasn't going to leave home and go back to being an employee. Martin Slagter (former European head of Dell computers) was just setting up a network of women at home selling computers. I became his first agent. I ended up recruiting and training 630 agents. I would be demonstrating family computing with the Usborne book and CDs, but I did it all from home, with the kids around me. When I got pregnant with my third child it got too much – you had to carry these computers around. PC World came into the market at this time and suddenly everyone was using us to demonstrate the machines and then buying cheaper computers at PC World. So it fell apart.

"Meanwhile, Thomas was selling the first online auction site to Mercedes (this was pre-eBay). I thought, 'Wait a minute, this internet thing is about connecting people, it's not about a new sales channel.' I just got really excited again about the idea of people supporting people. We were sitting in Pizza Express with three kids under five, all throwing food about, and I said, 'Could I set up a networking site like a Yahoo forum but for businesses from all over the world?' And Thomas said that's a really good idea. So I did it.

"It was 1998. I found a computer expert to write it and Ecademy was born."

Collapse

"I set up an online community from home. I mentioned it to someone over lunch one day and he said, 'I want to put £250,000 into that idea.' He wanted 50 percent of the shares and I agreed. That got me the money to design the website. I was into connecting people. But he was into the financial return. He took it all the way through to the stock market and in March 2000 we were worth £22 million on paper. We were six weeks from the flotation. We were in the queue behind Lastminute.com. And then it crashed. The investor wasn't interested anymore and we bought his shares back.

"We went into massive debt," recalls Penny. "We called it 'castle to caravan.' Thomas and I just looked at each other. 'What do we do, close down Ecademy?' But we had a really thriving community of business people. A lot of them, because of the dot-com crash, lost their businesses. There was no Facebook, LinkedIn or Twitter, so they were relying on Ecademy for their support network. If we'd just turned it off that would have been really selfish.

"We made the decision to go into funding it ourselves and by pouring in our own money we ultimately lost our house. It was a horrible time for three or four years. We were just bringing it around when Facebook, Twitter and LinkedIn emerged. But they were all highly funded from Silicon Valley. Facebook had £2.5 billion, so they could make it free. But the Ecademy model was £10 subscription a month and our business model was ripped apart by them.

"At that point Ecademy really became more of a social enterprise for us. It became our love and we knew we had to make our money elsewhere to support it. We adored our Ecademy community. We always believed it had asset value, but not income value. It was then that I started to learn the difference between income and equity. And that's really the shift from being a business person to an entrepreneur. It was at this point that I started other companies."

Present day

Ecademy is now a global community of owners of small businesses, and Penny speaks regularly at high-profile business conferences. She also advises small business owners through her support of programmes like the Key Person of Influence Program and the MasterMind Agency. Had the dot-com crash not happened, Penny could have been an idle millionaire in her thirties. She came very close to huge financial success. Is she downhearted?

"If the £22 million flotation had gone through, I don't believe my children would have been brought up with the level of grounding, learning and values around hard work and contribution that they have received. My kids have been through serious disruption. They were all at private schools and a lot of their friends were from very wealthy families. I had to disconnect from that world because I could not keep up with the social life and material possessions that were a priority to many of them. None of the women worked and so they didn't understand how hard it was to be able to afford this Italian meal we'd gone out for and I just couldn't cope with it. 'Are you coming skiing with us?' 'No,' I'd reply, 'not this time.'

"One of my friends said recently, 'We were all talking about you. You were the only working mother and we all decided that your children are so much better than ours. Ours are lazy, disconnected from reality. We were saying how driven and lovely your kids are.' My kids worked Saturdays and they worked in their gap years. In this world it's not good for your children if they haven't got the skills to get out there. They don't know how to overcome adversity, cope with uncertainty and failure. Our kids have seen us work really hard and manage our way through a lot."

Penny has combined and integrated her home and work life whenever possible. "We also had a great time. We met all our Ecademy members in California – we hired a Winnebago for five weeks. We travelled to Asia with the children meeting members. They were four years old with their Ecademy badges, shaking hands with people. In March 1999 we had our first Ecademy meeting at the Institute of Directors in Pall Mall. We asked if anyone fancied an offline meeting and 27 members came along. We had a corner in the wine bar and I stood on a crate and said, 'This is fun, I wonder if we can get something going here. If you enjoyed this, come again – but next time bring one person with you.' Within nine months we had 400 people at events. A big web company called Scient flew Chris Lochhead over. They paid us £20,000 to speak at our event – it was incredible."

Penny's biggest challenge

"Internet trolls! We had about 17 members who were total bullies. Whenever a new member came in they would mock them. If one of them had an opinion, someone else would challenge it. They drove many people away. We had about 200,000 members at that point. LinkedIn was only doing a little. Twitter didn't exist, and Facebook was for students. So they only had Ecademy. It was like the only pub in town that the alcoholic could go to. I had these trolls psychologically profiled and they were displaying signs of mental disturbance. In the end we had to ban them all. That's when they decided to sabotage the business. We had to contact the police because one of them started contacting the children. It got really nasty and we moved house.

"At the bottom of the Ecademy site it says 'safe networking' – we pledged that we would look after and protect people, and it made us niche. It's easy to be big if you say anything goes. We believe the internet should have a safe corner where you can have opinions and be reasonably treated."

Penny's biggest success

"The Digital Youth Academy. I had the lightbulb moment in 2011. While looking at apprenticeships, youth unemployment, problems with companies embracing digital properly, the economic downturn – I wondered, couldn't we create a new kind of apprenticeship in the UK? Could we get a young person into a company via an apprenticeship, and encourage digital? Many colleges now run the Social Digital Apprenticeship and place apprentices into companies. We have a lot of different countries contacting us about the Digital Youth Academy wanting to license it, so it's going to be global."

What would Penny have done differently?

"I'd have found a business partner earlier. My business partner now owns the second-largest coaching company outside of America. He's been coaching me. If I'd actually invested in one earlier, I could have got much further, much sooner."

What does Penny wish she'd known before starting out?

"I wish I'd known how long it would take. It's a long game. People get seduced by Dragons' Den. One of my mentees is 31. She wants to be a millionaire by the end of the year. You're putting yourself under so much stress. Life's a journey, not a destination. It might take fifteen years and if you're going to live with this level of adrenalin you're not going to do it! Most businesses are built organically, providing real value to real customers."

Penny's attitude to the recession

"I think we're beginning to really see it bite now and behaviour is changing. People are getting really hungry. Some people get aggressive when they're hungry. For Ecademy it's been really good. People realise the importance of connecting within other business communities who have similar values. So Ecademy membership has seen some benefits.

"The recession has really highlighted the youth disconnect from business. I think there would have been a youth unemployment

Penny's Secrets
TO DREAM BUSINESS SUCCESS

"

1 A big skill now is knowing how to create followers rather than just customers. I think people who know how to create followers are people who believe in their values, their ideas, and who can collaborate.

2 I have a mantra, that I'm an animal looking for food. A lot of people think that food should be brought to them, but my instinct is to say why shouldn't I have to get up every day and look for food? That's what most free animals do. The animals that don't are in cages.

3 You have to know what you're willing to sacrifice. One thing I won't sacrifice is my time with my kids. Know what your priorities are.

4 Really understand how your business contributes to people. If your business doesn't add real value to people now – it's very difficult to get attention. It's not enough to say you're a life coach – what's your unique value?

5 You've got to have technology skills – social media, software, mobile, Dropbox, Basecamp, Google Plus, etc. As soon as I step out of my office I'm as productive on the train in between meetings as I am at home.

"

problem anyway, because they are not understood by the business community well enough, low-skilled jobs are being removed by technology. And yet these young people could add a level of digital innovation to businesses that would be a form of 'data manufacturing.' They've been brought up digitally and have a different approach to life – which a lot of business owners don't appreciate. I actually think the recession has been good for me, because I want to create solutions to problems. But for people who stay doing the same thing, and are not meeting different people, or having different thoughts – then it's going to be hell."

> *I don't believe that there's anything that can't be done – there's always a way or a person that can do it. That's why I love networking. Through networking you find the right person and make things happen.*

Gina Romero

GINA SET UP the first business networking company for women in Singapore and promotes it online. When she started out she was petrified of networking – "I was so nervous I knocked over a bottle of wine" – but she is now described as "networking royalty" and has a loyal band of subscribers and followers.

DREAM BUSINESS OWNER

Gina Romero
Master franchise owner,
Athena Network,
Singapore

JOURNEY

Long-haul stewardess ➡ Entrepreneur

Gina acquired her first business experience as a teenager on the family pig farm in the Philippines. Her parents had left their jobs as domestic staff in recession-hit London in the 1980s to set up this new venture. "My mum came from a rural village. But my parents had no background in pig farming whatsoever," laughs Gina. "So it was kind of mad. I was pretty young and it was all a big adventure for me."

Gina learnt some business basics whilst helping to manage the farm. In order to raise more cash for hungry pigs, her parents returned to the UK to work and sent money back to build the capital for the farm. Gina stayed with the farm manager and continued her school studies to be a vet.

It was then that nearby Mount Pinatubo erupted, killing more than 800 people and ending countless livelihoods – including that of Gina and her family.

Catastrophe

"The volcano was only 11 miles from where we were. A lot of the buildings collapsed and we lost our stock and we had to reinvest and rebuild the roofs. That created extra cost and there's no insurance for that type of thing. But what really killed the business was the fact the surrounding areas were buried in mud. We couldn't carry on. My parents had to go back to the UK. Mum went to work but Dad had nowhere to live and went into a hostel for the homeless.

"I was stuck in the Philippines and not entitled to any help. I had to sell off what was left of the equipment. I didn't know what to do with myself, to be honest. Everything had been turned upside down. I didn't have time to plan anything."

With her life in turmoil, Gina took a flight back to London. "On the aeroplane I remembered a childhood dream about wanting to be crew on an airline – and I decided I'd apply for an airline job. It would be fun, I could travel around and earn some money. I sat on the flight thinking, 'Yes, I can do this.'"

But British Airways said no. Gina was too young and needed to re-apply. In the interim she got a job in a currency exchange.

"It paid really badly and there was no career progression. But to me it was a stepping stone to getting a job in BA and was more relevant than working in retail or something else. Because I don't have a degree, I've always had to work a lot harder to build up my profile. It was a strategic move on my part. I knew I'd be up against a lot of competition at BA so I did a lot of research in finding out how I could get an airline job. I got it eventually and ended up working for BA for ten years."

Life change

Gina went on to meet her future husband. They bought a house together and got married. They both had jobs and Gina was happy flying.

But you can't control everything in life. Five months after their wedding, with Gina three months pregnant, her husband had a devastating car accident.

"When I got to the hospital the doctors said, 'If he survives the next four hours we may have some hope.' He was in a coma for a month. He came out of hospital in a wheelchair and I was seven months pregnant. Whilst he'd done fantastically well and proved the doctors wrong, he was left brain-damaged and he couldn't dress or feed himself. Then I had the baby and him to care for. I was in complete denial. I was assuming that everything was going to go back to normal eventually.

"Then a year later it finally hit me. It wasn't going to happen. I felt so trapped and alone. Everyone was telling me how lucky I was. People didn't appreciate how difficult it was. I was very depressed at this point in my life."

Over time the marriage broke down and they split up. Then Gina developed a new relationship with Bobby, a family friend who helped her dad with his IT problems. "Only Bobby knew how depressed I was. One of the things that was on my mind constantly was the fact that I really wanted to have another baby and now I wouldn't be able to. I didn't want my son to be on his own and have to go through something like this. I was an only child, and I felt that if I'd had a sister it would have helped me through." The relationship with Bobby was a new start and, for Gina, it was like beginning a new life.

A new business venture

The divorce meant Gina needed extra money to pay for the mortgage and a second child that she went on to have with Bobby. He came up with an idea of buying secondhand laptops, wiping the data, cleaning them up and reselling them. At a time when new laptops were very expensive there was a huge demand for second-hand ones.

They started putting the laptops on eBay, and the response was so great they were putting the children to bed and working until the early hours and at weekends. They hadn't planned for this level of demand.

Bobby's IT expertise and Gina's outstanding customer service meant they were able to compete with bigger companies. "I was working from the house, changing nappies on the floor, looking after my toddler, answering emails all day and picking up calls. Bobby would come home from his day job and start physically cleaning and preparing these laptops, and customers would sometimes come and collect them.

"We were earning way more than Bobby's salary. He needed to decide if he was going to leave his job or not. He's less of a risk-taker than I am and he wasn't sure. So I went back to BA part-time, but I was now a completely different person. I used the opportunity to relax a bit. I had the most up-to-date phone – only the pilots had these phones. My colleagues didn't know I was running a business remotely."

Flying also enabled Gina to see the trends happening abroad. They got very excited about Wi-Fi after Gina saw it in New York. They tried it at home.

"We got amazingly far with the Wi-Fi idea and this proved to be my biggest success – and my biggest blunder. We experimented with a friend's flat in Kingston to get the whole building connected to Wi-Fi." Gina set up a demo, recruited her friends, borrowed laptops, hired plinths and created a really lovely event in the lobby of the building.

"I hosted it like a party. We had cheese and wine. We had to dangle the router out the window. It was such a precarious setup but it worked. All these laptops were all online. I had my dodgy suit, badge and TipTop Laptop business cards – we must have looked like a pair of rookies!

"Then, during the demo, this guy walks through the lobby in an immaculate striped suit with a red handkerchief in the pocket. He turned out to be the Managing Director (who owned the building we were in, along with a chain of others). He said he was actually meeting a wireless company who'd quoted five million to install Wi-Fi in all the buildings. I gave him this dog-eared business card. God knows what he thought. He said he'd really like to talk more about this and then he left. The following morning he rang to arrange a meeting the following day at 7.30 am.

"I went to that meeting in the same suit, as I only had the one! I was really excited but on the other hand we were clueless. We didn't know anything about what we were getting into. We sat down with this guy who asked us loads of questions. He was fascinated with our energy and enthusiasm. He said, 'I love it – send me a proposal.' Fine, we said, but we didn't even know what a proposal was! We got on the internet, found out what it was and how to do it."

Learning from mistakes

Gina and Bobby were asked to run a Wi-Fi pilot for six months. They felt totally out of their depth. Gina was constantly looking up information online about wiring up the building. But the pilot ran successfully and they got called back in by the MD who loved it and wanted them to install Wi-Fi in all their buildings and asked them to come in with costings.

"This is where it all went horribly wrong. I did have a business adviser and I sat down with him and he helped us put the pricing model together – my weakest area – and worked out the costs. We offered it at £10 per month – on the basis of 100 percent uptake – and that made £20 profit per unit sold.

"We put it to them and assumed they would buy it. But they wanted us to install it. *And* sell it. It was our Dragons' Den moment when it all goes pear-shaped. I can remember that feeling that it sounded really dangerous. It's OK for them. They have nothing to lose. It means if we get only 50 percent take-up we're going to lose money. My biggest concern was if the cost of broadband went down then we would have to compete with BT. I said it wasn't going to work. They said, 'That's the offer.'

"I decided not to bring our business adviser back into the boardroom with us to negotiate. And left to my own devices, I panicked and screwed the negotiation up. When they put the deal on the table I said 'No.' But I didn't know how to negotiate a better deal. I was out of my depth. I said, 'Sorry, it's not a good deal for us,' and closed the book on it.

"My mistake was to not bring in our adviser. They really wanted what we were offering, and there would have been room to negotiate. All the big companies like Facebook always put a guy in to manage their interests so the people behind the idea don't mess it up. Entrepreneurs don't necessarily know how to manage the business."

Developing the business

After this disappointing outcome, Gina looked to grow her business in other ways. They moved out of their garage and into offices. Networking provided the key to evolving their business. "I was so new to the game, I didn't even know about networking. But a random call come through to our new office inviting me to a business network for women.

"I went along without any expectations. But I really enjoyed it, and at the end someone gave a testimonial for TipTop Laptops and said we were brilliant. It turned out that, by coincidence, a woman had bought a laptop from us on eBay and been so happy with our service. I talked to her afterwards and she was a web designer who had just started her own company. I decided to carry on attending as a member."

The networking group proved invaluable to Gina as she began to rethink the business.

"I love the AA – I love how it doesn't matter what car you're in they'll come out and help you if you're a member. They service the person, not the car. To me that's genius. I thought, why can't IT be like that? It was so labour-intensive – going out and counting out all the computers, servers and printers. I had this revelation that we would sell IT support for people, not machines. Package it like the airlines – you get to pick the class according to your needs: Economy, Executive or Director."

"I also started to ask myself why we weren't making enough money even though we were working so hard. I just kept thinking, who would spend a lot of money on IT? And where are they based? I visualised my target customer: he's rich, he's wearing his Armani suit, he drives a Porsche, his business is in Mayfair. I realised I have been totally mis-selling my business. My husband has a technical background and he's very talented. I have a background in customer service and we can service very high-end clients.

"I decided we were looking for small companies with five to eleven staff who were based in the West End of London, who had a high turnover and who considered IT to be critical to their business. Investment banks! They lose millions if their IT doesn't work. I was fired up. I re-did the website. I started targeting private investment banking firms – calling ourselves a boutique tech solutions company.

"The results were pretty much immediate. Jess, the website designer, had a really good referral for me."

Gina put on her suit again. "I felt I was dressing for a part that wasn't my real role, and I still feel like that a lot of the time, but I realise that's a part of stepping up. It's just about stretching yourself to be a little bit better than you already are. But now I accept that as normal. For a lot of my business career I struggled with authenticity – I felt I was faking it and conning people all the time. Even when I went to Athena I'd stand up and say all this stuff and I believed it but the voice in my head was saying, 'But you've never serviced one of those clients before – can you really do it?' I didn't listen!

"Their IT was in such a terrible state. We fixed it and they were really happy. And through that we generated two more clients. Our turnover increased from £25,000 a year initially to £150,000, and then up to £500,000."

Nightmare

Gina and Bobby's main client was expanding rapidly, growing to 200 staff within 18 months. New recruits were constantly contacting Gina. There was no system internally within the company and one of the new recruits wanted to replace them with a bigger firm. They had nights of endless worry and stress. It was no longer any fun. But they knew that if they lost their client, they would also lose their house and their business.

"We were earning more and more money but getting increasingly in trouble with cash flow. We were ordering £2000 laptops for all of their new staff. They were hiring five people a week and we were scared to lose the business. We had always worked hard but never experienced this sort of stress. We'd always dealt with the CEO before, who would sign off our work sheets so we got paid. Now we had layers of people to deal with, people who just didn't understand our relationship with the company. So we were putting in the work sheets, but they wouldn't be signed off. We would lie in bed at night worrying.

"I'd never felt so trapped in my life. I remember hearing my heart thumping with all the stress and anxiety. One night Bobby and I were lying in bed talking and the sun was coming up. I realised we'd been awake all night long worrying. I couldn't do it anymore. I said to Bobby, 'I can't live like this. We're young enough to start again. I'm sick of them controlling us, I'm sick of being scared and sick of lying awake worrying. You know we started with one laptop. Let's start with one laptop again. We'll do it differently.' He looked at me and said, 'Alright. Let's do it.'

"I got out of bed that morning and felt like I'd won the lottery. I felt like I was floating two feet off the ground. We sat down with Renita from our client, and told her. She sat tapping her pencil for a few minutes and then asked if there was anything they could do to renegotiate the deal. We said we were sorry, but no. So we left. We went home on top of the world.

"But just as we were crossing the road, Bobby's phone rang: the company wanted to hire him. He saw the potential to play with someone else's IT budget – buy all the things he didn't have and work on big projects. He was really keen and I couldn't put him off."

Starting again: an Athena franchise

"Bobby's pay increase allowed me not to have to work anymore. However, I was so bored, so quickly, to the point that I was completely miserable!"

So, having wound down the IT business, and then worked for a year with the Athena network's head office, Gina started again and took up her own Athena franchise. "I spent a year setting up and marketing. I launched three groups in the UK and I was just about to launch my fourth when Bobby's head office moved to Singapore." So Gina decided to start up an Athena franchise in Singapore.

There she met Clare, who became her co-founder. Gina didn't plan to start networking in a big way. She wanted time with her children. So they planned to start with a coffee morning with 15 people.

"Clare didn't know what she was getting herself into! We had 150 people sign up for that coffee morning. All I did was go on Twitter. It just spread through Facebook and word of mouth like wildfire. And now we've got 11,000 likes on our Singapore Facebook page."

Gina's mistakes

"Yes, Bobby and I made many mistakes. Because we were earning lots of money, and I had a stack of invoices, and I'd given receipts to everyone, in my mind we were a proper business. But, really, we weren't. Bobby and I just didn't know what we were doing. We had so much to find out – taxes and so on." So they contacted Business Link, and Gina went on a business start-up workshop.

Why was Gina successful?

"What made it work was the combination of Bobby and me, a geek and a people person. As we advanced we went from TipTop

Laptops to TipTop Technologies. And then we started to style ourselves as a boutique IT company. Other companies said it couldn't be done. For Bobby and me, 'can't be done' was the best thing we'd ever heard, because we both don't believe that there's anything that can't be done. There's a way, or a person who can do it. And that's why I love networking, because I know it can be done – you just need the right person. Or the right idea. Or the right solution. Everything can be done and that's how I think we set ourselves apart."

What does Gina wish she'd known before starting out

"I would have surrounded myself with expertise in the areas I'm not good at. I spent so many years struggling to do things like finance and cash flow which made my life extremely difficult. Now I don't do any of the stuff I don't like or I'm no good at. I surround myself with a community of resources."

Networking

"I was very strategic about the way I was networking. I was very specific about whom I met and the benefit they would get out of it. I created champions who were out there spreading the word. I looked for people who were very influential on social media, who had a lot of followers. And I met with the heads of organisations for women. I went to the SCWO, which is the national coordinating body of women's organisations in Singapore. I didn't want to be seen as the competition to the local organisations, so I went and met them and told them what I was going to do and volunteered to do their social media. I give them a half-day a month to do whatever they needed. And in return they introduced me to the board members of the women's organisations over here."

Gina openly admits she was a technophobe. The attraction of social media is her love of communication and connecting with people. "I went onto Twitter and within a month I had 1500 followers. It's just engaging with people. Everyone is very reserved over here, whereas I blurt everything out! And they seem to love that."

Gina's Secrets
TO DREAM BUSINESS SUCCESS

66

1 Get your business model right. Our IT business was just not scalable – that was the problem.

2 Know what you want to get at the end of your business. Some people set up a business and they don't know why – if you're looking for flexibility and more time with the family, don't start an IT support business!

3 People say to me, you're in a male-dominated world. People say, what about the recession? Sorry, I just carry on with what I'm doing. If you keep your eye on what you're trying to achieve and keep re-adjusting your strategy along the way, these factors shouldn't really affect you. Find your way around them.

99

COACHING TIPS #9

Do's and Don'ts of networking: It's not what you know …

OK, let's get this straight from the start. Nobody likes networking. That is, initially.

I have known hard-bitten hacks who have grilled politicians and stood on the frontlines of war to bolt from networking groups the moment they heard the roar behind the door.

When you think about it, trying to ingratiate yourself, make an impact or, heavens above, sell to a room full of strangers is enough to bring you out in hives. But that's where most people make their first fatal error. You don't have to do any of the above.

Networking is all about getting you and your business in other people's consciousness. How you do this should feel comfortable and enjoyable to you. So from the outset try to source a networking group that suits your needs and feels right.

Morning breakfast clubs are great for early risers but a nightmare if you have kids' lunchboxes and school runs to juggle. Lunchtime groups from noon to 2 pm usually fit in well with women, while evening groups generally work for all.

Go to a few before you decide. Size up the members – are they like you or your potential clients? Was the welcome you received warm and professional? Is the group structured and business-focused? Can you see real business being done between the members?

Most networking groups offer membership schemes and you will be expected to commit to the group and attend regularly. You may be required to introduce yourself and your business with a short presentation. Don't worry – everyone loathes these to begin with but pretty soon you get the knack of doing them.

There are also specialist groups. Networking for gay lawyers, women in journalism and PR, writers and artists, hospitality and entertainment workers, coaches, healers – do your research, and you'll find there is a group out there just right for you.

Now here's the really great part about networking. You will meet people who inspire, who can help you build and develop your business; you get support and contacts; you feel less isolated (if you work alone); and you even make really good friends. And yes, you *will* get business from it too. In short you will grow.

However, there is a way to go about networking to make it work for you. It's not an excuse to stand in a corner clutching a drink and monopolising the one person who you do know there. Nor is it a social date where you have a lovely lunch and go back to work sloshed with a bulging pocket of business cards.

And it is definitely *not* an occasion for the hard sell. Nothing clears a room faster than a pushy sales person forcing their wares on anything with a pulse that crosses their path.

Networking can be an enjoyable and powerful way of raising your business profile and gaining clients but you have to know what you are doing or it can become a stressful nightmare.

The wallflower's guide to working the room

No matter whether you are an introvert, an extrovert or an ambivert (a bit of both), you can network in a way to suit your style. Here are some tips to ensure you and your business make the right impact:

- Look the part. You are your brand, so look well-groomed, up to date and attractive. You are your business' shop window – so are you Harrods or Primark? Check for clean shoes and nails, dandruff on collar and if in doubt invest a couple of hours with an image consultant to get it right.

- Make good eye contact and give a warm, firm handshake, not a limp or knuckle-crushing one.

- Smile and let it light your eyes. There is an old Chinese saying, "A miserable man should never open a shop." People who smile put others at ease.

- Listen, listen, listen – our ears never get us into trouble. Find out what people do, how you can help them, who you know that they might know. Make it your business to use networking as a fact-finding mission about others, the market or new trends.

- Introduce them to others. Be known as a social fulcrum who connects people. It will make you look good and generous and it will come back to you.

- Ask people if they know anyone who would benefit from what you do. Describe your ideal client to them.

- Be interested in others before talking about yourself.

- Don't rule people out because they look shy, different, introverted or are in a profession completely alien to what you seek. You never know who they know.

- If you get stuck with an Olympian bore, don't stay put out of politeness. Say "We need to mingle" and do just that.

- When presented with someone's business card, show courtesy by holding it in both hands and reading it carefully and then commenting on it before putting it respectfully away. Afterwards you can write on the back what you talked about. People's business cards reflect who they are, so treat them well.

- Always follow up after a networking session. Email those you met and say how nice it was to meet them and maybe even suggest a coffee if you feel that would be useful.

- Repeat all of the above. One trip to a networking event will yield little. You need to go again so people get used to seeing you, understand more about what you do and then do business with you.

They say it takes five visits to the same networking group before people fully get what you do and start to trust you and refer clients on. It is worth the investment and your business will significantly benefit from you getting out of your comfort zone and connecting with others.

CHAPTER 10

Dynamic double acts

“If we're together nothing is impossible.”

Winston Churchill

"You mustn't underestimate the power of two."

Rosie Wolfenden

ROSIE WOLFENDEN and Harriet Vine – awarded MBEs in 2013 for services to the fashion industry – met as students at Chelsea College of Art. "I was living with my sister," explains Rosie, "and our roof fell in. I didn't know what to do. So I rang up Harriet and she had a spare room. She was looking for a new flatmate and I moved in the next day. We got on so well and had loads of fun. When we graduated, we organised a party. We designed the invites, negotiated a better price and got free drinks for everyone. And we made a small profit! I love having an idea and making it happen. I love creating something from nothing."

DREAM BUSINESS OWNER

Rosie Wolfenden
Co-founder,
Tatty Devine, UK

JOURNEY

Art student ➜ Creator of tongue-in-cheek jewellery

One night Harriet was walking home when, outside a furniture shop, she found 14 bin-liners of leather sample books. She knew they'd be good for something. "We were students," says Rosie, "and we lived off very little and we always collected free stuff. We had an art student mentality – we were in and out of skips, scavenging and gleaning the streets for treasures. I spent my childhood collecting stones off the beach.

"Lo and behold, we started making the leather sample books into wrist bands. Then we took them to Portobello Market. It was a steep learning curve, but everything is there for you to grasp and learn – product, customers, costings, competition. We made £50. So with that we did the next Saturday and we made £300. And we kept selling on the market stall. We literally started with nothing – well a student debt and overdrafts. In July 1999, Harriet rang Camden Council and we did Spitalfields as well. We made £60 the first day. It felt really good. We just put our stuff on our colourful table – no market research – and sold things for what we thought was right. Within three weeks there were two other stalls selling the same thing. We had a range of colours because we had the sample book but they only had white. It made us realise we had a real, viable product.

"It was such hell to do. Getting up at 5 am and driving in my clapped-out Mini. You only got a pitch if you were a regular. So you'd queue with a name on a list and wait for someone to not turn up. You didn't get told if you'd got a stall until 9 am. I'd sleep for three hours in my car and then I'd be at the pitch until 7 pm. It was a long day. But it was always worth it. We'd meet stylists there. Urban Outfitters bought us from there. It was so exciting."

In September 1999, Rosie went on holiday. While she was away she phoned Harriet and heard that interest from buyers had continued. Then Harriet asked Rosie if she wanted to go into business with her. And of course she said yes.

"There'd been a real drought of fun stuff in the 90s. Everything had got very serious. Everything that we made, we made so that *we* could wear it. When we couldn't find anything we wanted to wear, we made it. No one had heard of customising clothes in the late 90s, but we were cutting up sweatshirts and t-shirts and sewing them back together, getting old duvets of cartoon characters and making them into skirts. We just wanted to wear them and have fun and show off and stand out.

"I was also working at Steinberg & Tolkien, a vintage shop on the King's Road. High-profile stylists come in there, and I'd help them select stuff for shoots. So I soon understood their requirements. A stylist for *Vogue* came into the shop and I was wearing this thing on my head which Harriet and I had made just as an experiment. She said, 'I love that thing on your head. Can I use it for my Millennium shoot? Where's it from?' 'Oh,' I said, 'my company makes it.' 'Well, bring your collection in on Monday.' But we didn't have a collection! So we made one that weekend. Harriet's mum was a seamstress – the type of person who can hand-sew a garment and it comes out perfect. She came up with her sewing machine and helped us make a collection out of all the bits and pieces we had."

Tatty Devine

As their business took shape, Harriet had been trying to think of a name. They had various suggestions and one day Rosie suggested 'Tatty Devine.' The name worked immediately. Rosie spoke to a shop and tried it out and they said, "Oh yes, I've heard of you." Of course they hadn't – it had only just been invented!

"A friend knew the press officer at Whistles and introduced us. And soon Tatty Devine was in the *Evening Standard* – and then

Vogue. I got home one day and my flatmate said, 'I'm not your secretary, but Harvey Nichols just rang.' Money was coming in. We thought, 'Wow, we can get a studio!' We found a shop in Brick Lane. The toilet was blocked up with concrete, everything about it was disgusting, but we got it really cheap. Harriet's dad, a builder, put a floor down, we rolled our sleeves up and we made it what it is. And in January we moved in. There was no turning back. And we've been there 12 years now."

The shop proved a powerful tool. It allowed Rosie and Harriet to slap their identity all over it. But they also held lots of events there, events which drew in their friends, artists, filmmakers, musicians. These gatherings also meant they could meet their customers and find out what they thought and what they really wanted.

"When we got our shop it enabled people to experience our ideas, our aesthetic. I think that was really important because word of mouth is really important. You've got to get out there and be seen – whether it's a trade show, a shop or a website, it's a meeting place and that's key."

The next step

"The core customers love what we do, they don't want us to get any bigger and they don't want us to 'sell out.' That's the challenge now – how do we keep our integrity but still grow?

"It's all about turning the page and getting to the next stage. Six years ago I should have gone on a business course to learn all the things I'm learning about now. I wouldn't have changed the beginning because it was really important and it laid the foundations and informed what we do. No one can ever take away how much fun we had and that free-spiritedness."

Rosie's biggest challenge

"Two or three years ago we sat down and said, 'Right, we're going to work really hard, and we're going to make this business work.' That's been the biggest challenge, trying to fine-tune everything so as to become a serious business. We're no longer doing everything by gut instinct.

"For example, it's really important that our website is contemporary, and it's got to be doing the right things. There's a girl who's always done our website. We've employed her for seven years, and she taught herself how to make a website. It's always been like that, really grassroots, home-made. But we decided we'd better get an outsider in to help her, someone who understands branding, the current market, what websites should look like. So we've done that, she's had to learn and re-adjust, and she has. She's such an important part of the team."

Rosie's biggest success

"We've grown 50 percent in the last year and I put a lot of that down to being in Selfridges in Oxford Street. It created this huge brand awareness. And taking our laser cutter into the shop gave customers such an experience. With most people shopping online these days, the customer experience has got to be paramount. The buyer at Selfridges suggested bringing the laser cutter into the shop for a day. We said we could bring it in for two months.

What I love is that we employ girls who are so clever and creative, and they are multitasking to such an amazing level. They run the machinery, they make the jewellery, they talk to the customers, they live and breathe the brand.

"That makes me really proud of what we're doing. To be able to share with the customer that experience and for the customer to see a bespoke thing being made in a department store there and then is special on every level.

"We're still trying to work out exactly where we want to take the business. But we've got 30 members of staff, and it's kicked in that it has got to make money now. Our staff love the product, and they understand that it's not just about making money, but we need, and want, to create wealth through it. It has to be about money because we pay 12 mortgages, five babies have been born, and it's 30 people's livelihoods on the line!"

What has made Rosie successful?

"It never occurred to me that I would ever work for anyone. My mentality was always to make my own money. When I was 12 I set up a business while I was working in a hotel in France. I bought some inflatable mattresses and charged people ten francs to borrow them to go down the river rapids.

"Next, there's the fact that my father's business failed. I know how awful that failure was. I think that makes me quite determined. There's an anxiety at the thought of failure.

"Then there's authenticity. We've got this business because of its authenticity. We believe in originality and integrity and Tatty Devine is loved because of that.

"Finally, there's knowing what you want. We started organically and honestly, and we put all the fun of our spirit into it. We simply had a passion. It wasn't financially driven. OK, we had to write a business plan to get our bank account and an overdraft, but much more important was knowing what we wanted."

Rosie's attitude to the recession

"During the Recession we did well, we exploded. I put it down to the lipstick effect. People are still spending £15–30 on something special for themselves to perk them up. Our product makes people smile. It's affordable, it's English, and it's quality.

"I'm very optimistic. Yes, I question everything, but I always presume that we'll be OK. When I go to buyers, I always think they'll buy it. I wouldn't go if I didn't think they'd buy it."

How important is social networking to Rosie?

"The word 'networking' used to be horrific to us. We never thought we'd do such a thing. Now I quite enjoy it. Twitter allows us to share everything. It can go against you as much as for you, but I think you have to embrace it. It's so important in terms of communicating with our customers. Someone copied us. We tweeted about it and put up a blog. We checked with our lawyers we weren't being libellous. Within 12 hours we had 2000 tweets. It was trending on Twitter. Everyone contacted us and it suddenly felt like we had an army out there on our behalf."

Rosie's attitude to dynamic double acts

"You mustn't underestimate the power of two. Our different skill sets have been key to staying sane and not driving our partners mental. We flow together.

"We talk to each other about ideas, themes, topics. But then Harriet sits down and looks at techniques and materials and draws up the ideas and works very closely with the product. I step back, get on with running the business and then help Harriet to edit once the collection is finished. The editing is a nightmare. We make 150 products and we really only want 50.

"With two of us, we can have a conversation. You can only solve a problem when you voice it – you can't do it in your own head. We can ask each other anything. Just the nature of asking can help solve a problem. If you're on your own you've got to make sure you talk to your friends, family, business adviser, local business agency, somebody like-minded you can bounce ideas off.

"We've never had to get permission for anything from anyone – we only have to get permission from each other and we rarely say no.

"The advantages of being in a partnership are having someone to talk to and someone to share the responsibility. Harriet and I are very lucky because we've always had a lot of trust and faith in each other. We've been together 13 years and it's stronger than it's ever been. There have never been times of not getting on. You're in a parental role when you have employees.

Rosie's Secrets
TO DREAM BUSINESS SUCCESS

66

1 Love what you do. It's very difficult to sell something if you don't like it. Whether you're selling a service, a product or an idea, you've got to really believe in it, otherwise no one else is going to believe in it.

2 Never forget that it's a two-way street. You have stuff to sell and people need to buy stuff. People who make products are often so shy about walking into a store and saying, 'You should be selling this.' You've got to believe in it. People used to ask me, 'How do you get so much press?' I'd go through magazines, see who the stylist was, ring them up and ask to come and see them. They need stuff to put in their magazines. They need stories, they need content, they need products – and they're usually quite lazy! So if you go to them with content they're very grateful.

3 You need a space to operate from, whether it's a physical space or a website, because you have to be able to share everything. You have to have a platform where people come and join you and interact with what you're doing. Or it could be that you go to trade shows and mingle with buyers, consumers, your competition.

Continued overleaf

"

4 Energy levels are really important. Harriet says I've got a ball of energy inside me. I need plenty of sleep – eight hours. To be confident, you need to be energetic and you don't have that if you're not well rested.

5 Think big. Bite off a little bit more than you can chew. You need to constantly struggle, be stretched, be motivated. Create more work for yourself.

6 If you're in partnership with someone else, the business name is really important. If it's your name and not the other person's name, it's really hard to deal with.

7 Doing a business plan shouldn't feel like homework, but should be a way to get excited about your business. It's so you understand what it is that you are doing and want to do. A business plan enables you to create a goal. And it's all intermingled – it's all one thing. If you're excited about your business you'll be writing a business plan in your sleep, you'll be thinking, 'Who do we want to work with next? What are we going to sell next? What are we going to do next? Who do we need to employ in order to realise all these dreams?'

"

" Holly and I would have coffees and talk intensely about the business. It was like a courtship, in which Holly finally asked me out! "

Sophie Cornish

LIKE ROSIE and Harriet, Sophie Cornish found her dream business partnership when she was invited by Holly Tucker to join her to set up a company.

Where it all started

Sophie had an entrepreneurial itch as a child. She recalls working out

DREAM BUSINESS OWNER

Sophie Cornish
Co-founder,
Notonthehighstreet.com,
UK

JOURNEY
Journalist ➡
Advertising ➡
Dot-com entrepreneur

her career at the age of 12 when she was already writing and selling magazines to friends. "Being an entrepreneur is in your blood," she says, "it's always there."

"I remember an uncle telling me that as a child he used to buy packs of Smarties on the way to school and then sell them individually. And this really impressed other people. What I remembered from his story wasn't the Smarties but the fact that other people were impressed by his entrepreneurial thinking."

Sophie knew she didn't want to go to university. "I just wanted to get on with it. And anyway, it's funny that in the environments where it matters, people often assume you already have a degree. But where it isn't required, well, it doesn't matter."

Her first job, at the age of 19, was working at *Cosmopolitan*. But while she loved it, it wasn't exactly what she wanted. "I had this dream job at *Cosmopolitan*. But I was really curious about the publishing and advertising side. Editorial was great but it was the commercial teams who were working out how to grow the business."

So Sophie moved to a branding company working for Boots cosmetics. "That gave me commercial thinking. And at 25 I got to decide what colour make-up we were going to have, what it was going to be called and packaged in. That was massive fun. And then I moved around until I settled into a six-year stint in advertising.

"I loved magazines and I found it relatively easy to get my writing published. People liked the stuff I wrote right from the beginning. But it was a double-edged sword. Writing was lovely and straightforward but a lot of things about it weren't right for me. It was business that I was interested in. What excited me was the idea of growing something out of nothing. I was always having ideas for businesses. It's what I did every night on the train on the way home. I knew friends who did the same.

"I had my son while I was working in advertising and returned to work full-time, which increasingly made me think I needed to work for myself. Then I had a second baby and didn't return."

Sophie went on to have various freelancing jobs, including with dot-com start-ups like WorldGallery.co.uk, selling prints and posters online. "It was very new and cool. It was a great time to get into the internet and I was very excited by it. I knew the owner would be fun and would do it well." It made Sophie very aware of one of the things that were essential in her life: working with fun, dynamic people.

She also worked at the online magazine, BEME.com. "IPC Media were invested in this and I had a job share as channel editor and writing for them. It was heavenly. You had a huge amount of freedom to do what you thought was right for the magazine. We had a budget. I had opportunity and autonomy. I was able to commission fun features that were daring. But the best thing was working with brilliant people."

After building up experience on these new websites, Sophie moved into an area she adored. A lover of all things beautiful and well-presented ("I am a perfectionist, I am Bree Van de Kamp"), she set up her own event and wedding styling business. She got married and then wrote a book about weddings.

"I loved Martha Stewart and the way she styled weddings. So that was my business – delivering to people who wanted that type of wedding. It was a long-term project. I did a floristry course. I worked unbelievably hard. But it just didn't bring the money in for the amount of time spent on it. It wasn't a scalable business."

It was disappointing, but it was an eye-opener and contributed to Sophie's business education.

Finding a partner

Undeterred, she began conversations about starting up other businesses with one or two like-minded friends. And one of them was Holly Tucker, who had been running small upmarket fairs. Holly's original concept was a real-life shopping fair, where partners would sell good-quality, unique products at upmarket London fairs like Barnes, Hampstead and Fulham. It proved incredibly successful – as long as it didn't rain.

Holly's formula worked, but the business needed to grow and develop in some way. It also became clear that the creative sellers wanted a new platform and way of selling. The new business formula was to stop live events and do the selling online instead.

After almost a year of plotting the business, on 2 January 2006, Holly and Sophie moved into their offices.

The start-up process

"As part of our research we talked to loads of people. Much of that was fruitful and worthwhile, because we spoke to many incredibly talented and experienced people. We needed someone to tell us if we were living in Cloud Cuckoo Land.

"And we had a financial plan – Holly's dad is an accountant, and now our CFO. (That doesn't mean just because your dad isn't an accountant you shouldn't have a CFO!) Having a detailed financial document is *essential*. You need to think the business through, anticipate the problems and have the advantage of having a heads-up. Investment only comes from having robust thinking and having tested the market and target audience. You have to thrash out what you need to do.

"We didn't have a mentor but we had many people who helped and guided us, like Tom Teichman from SPARK Ventures (who had invested in Lastminute.com). He had a feeling about us and the business. We did a serious presentation in order to get early-stage investment. Tom invested in us and has been a huge asset. He cares. He wants to see it succeed and we knew we needed investment. Our anticipated £40,000 start-up cost had already become £140,000!"

The horrific first year

"When we began, some things went wrong. With the press watching us, we launched the site and the checkout didn't work – we weren't transactional. Our mistake had been to out-source the website when we should have done it in-house from the beginning.

"We also had real financial problems. But we'd signed up new businesses and they needed us. They needed us to be successful and sell their products. They'd paid a reasonable fee and needed and expected sales immediately. We'd committed to advertising and marketing and there was absolutely no way we were going to give up on 100 businesses. Ninety percent of our businesses are run by women and they need them for money for their families. It was a hellish situation. There was an enormous expectation to match up to."

Holly had a new baby and Sophie already had two children, but they proceeded to work 16 hours a day, seven days a week. "It just took longer than we had planned for sales to pick up. But they did, and by the end of this year we will have turned over nearly £100 million in our business lifetime.

"For all the hard work, I feel grateful for doing what I do, and privileged. I also feel quite tired! It's given me a whole new career and now the business is in a really good place."

Sophie's biggest challenge

"The technical issues related to scaling and representing 3000 businesses. We now have a site that is totally different from the one we started with. There's been so much to learn – order management, having the products in the catalogue, uploading products, providing the support to the businesses. It continues to be a real sprint to keep up with the business, and the constant growth and change that comes with that.

"The day the site was meant to launch but had no checkout, we had to think on our feet. It was our first lesson in how running a business is about overcoming problems. We decided to run a promotion whereby if you left us your email address and let us contact you when we were transactional, we'd give you money to spend on the site. This turned out to be one of the best things that happened to us because had we not done that we wouldn't have captured all these visits. It actually gave us a headstart in getting a really substantial database growing right from day one."

Sophie's biggest success

"Our biggest success has been our rate of growth and our increase in revenue. We accept only 12 percent of people who apply to join. And huge numbers of customers shop with us each year. We have over 20 awards for entrepreneurship and customer service. But of course we're never satisfied."

What would Sophie have done differently?

"Our biggest mistake was outsourcing the website. I would have kept the technology in-house and invested more in marketing, especially digital marketing.

"But the real measure of a successful business person is not how they get straight from A to B without any hiccups along the way. It's about how they deal with the problems, how they overcome the sticky stuff."

Sophie's attitude to dynamic double acts

"Holly and I would have coffees and talk intensely about the business. It was like a courtship, in which Holly finally asked me out! I remember a cold shiver ran down my spine. It really was like a build-up to a date – it was in the air – and finally she sent me an email asking me if I would set up the business with her. I knew it was the most amazing opportunity. We were a great match. Holly is visionary and brilliant with money and, because of my advertising and journalism background, I knew what customers were looking for."

Sophie's Secrets
TO DREAM BUSINESS SUCCESS

"

1 You must have a business plan and do the financials with someone who can advise you.

2 Double the amount of money you think you'll need!

3 You must not be afraid.

4 You need a masochistic love of hard work, to be entrepreneurial and unnaturally passionate!

5 Finding the right business partner is fundamental.

6 Find the right team. You need to work with really talented people whom you value and trust.

7 You need to be doing it for the right reasons, a genuine belief in your business idea.

8 You should have a real affection and respect for the businesses you work with.

9 Your brand is an incredibly important part of the jigsaw puzzle. It's your relationship with the customer and what they see you as – how they decide whether to believe in you.

"

COACHING TIPS #10
Double your chances

At some point in your business you may be tempted to go into a partnership with someone who has a lot to offer and shares your passion. This is usually a sure sign that you are doing well and you have built up a reputation of trust and gravitas that is getting noticed by others.

Sharing a business can be hugely rewarding. You feel supported as the burdens of big decisions, the hard graft and the legwork are all shared by another person.

Making sure that your business partner is a good fit goes without saying but in many cases you won't know how good a fit they will be until you start working together. You may know friends and relatives you can trust who would seem like ideal candidates. But you risk deeply personal clashes, rifts and upsets that could have long-term repercussions going beyond business if you undertake such partnerships. Are you prepared for this?

Ideally your skills and experience should dovetail with your business partner's. If you are a creative visionary and marketing supremo there is no point going into business with someone similar. You need an opposite. Perhaps a forensic, detail-focused, project- and people-manager who excels at pulling together your business goals and who understands and shares your vision too.

Some like to be 'front of house,' others 'behind the scenes,' so be sure egos, needs and skills marry. And a marriage it surely is, as you will spend hours together working, planning, investing and developing. So be as sure as you can be that you have compatible skills and that you are driving to the same business outcome. You will see more of each other than your loved ones ever will.

Partnerships can be notoriously volatile – Simon and Garfunkel, Lennon and McCartney, Ray and Dave Davies of The Kinks – and sometimes the rifts are fatal. Trust and a dream shared are the two key components of a partnership.

From the outset it would be wise to draw up legal boundaries and your framework of responsibilities, and just like in a marriage, don't sign up if you're secretly hoping for the other person to change, to eventually fit in with your way of doing things or to dance to your tune. Transparency is paramount as are clear guidelines as to who is responsible for what.

Women going into business with other women must factor in child-care issues which could restrict working hours and commitment. Don't just think you can muddle through as this inevitably leads to one of the partners shouldering more of the load, which starts to create resentment.

Business karma

A less formal way of generating support as well as giving it is by gathering a team of associates and affiliates around you. These may be businesses that share some synchronicity with yours – e.g. a family lawyer could recommend a relationship or life coach to clients going through divorce cases. Or a florist might feature jewellers, candle-makers, chocolatiers or gift companies on its website as extras to be delivered with bouquets.

Mutual support can be negotiated via business referrals, shared programmes or packages, and the inclusion of your associates' and affiliates' URLs on websites benefits all when it comes to Google listings.

Be creative and you can gather a whole tribe of affiliated businesses who can cross-refer or support your business. For example, if you are a hypnotherapist you could have psychotherapists, acupuncturists, coaches, reflexologists, career counsellors, travel agents (flying phobias!), public-speaking experts and GPs in your stable of affiliates.

Don't necessarily see other people who are in the same business as you as your competitors or rivals. As you define and hone your offer it will be unique to you and again you can cross-refer customers and clients to others and create mutually supporting services.

Be generous. Pass leads or clients on to people you know. Be a fulcrum of connections and be sure to thank those who do the same for you.

Good business karma always comes back to you.

CHAPTER 11

Improve your sales
in 30 days

"Image and brand are everything."

Richard Branson
Meeting Myself Coming Back,
BBC Radio 4, 9 June 2012

66 Know your numbers – your profit margin and conversion rates. For example, if you want to earn £100,000, work out your average sale value. How many people do you need to see, how many sales do you need to make?99

Dylis Guyan

DYLIS GUYAN HAS spent a lifetime selling, and now provides her services to other people's companies. She describes her biggest success as "earning six figures in my first year of being self-employed."

DREAM BUSINESS OWNER

Dylis Guyan
IncreaseYourSalesin30days.com

JOURNEY

Corporate sales manager ➡ Business owner

Dylis was at the top of her game working for somebody else. In January 1999 she was standing on the podium with her sales team collecting awards and accolades. By August she had walked out of a job that she had absolutely loved for 14 years.

"Things had become horrible at work and I don't know why. But I looked at my options. I was not going to be treated like that. I could stay and fight, try and change the person involved, endure it or leave. The prospect of leaving made me very excited and at the same time very scared. I had a clear idea of what I wanted to do. But I listened to the people around me and tried once more to tackle the issue at work, but it was no good. Once my boss started the shouting, finger-pointing and clipboard-throwing, I knew I was never coming back.

"I was giving up a corporate environment and all its trappings: pension, car, a significant salary. It was not something to walk away from lightly. I'd just taken on a new mortgage as a single parent with two teenage children, but I was confident that I had the skills, knowledge and determination. I was driven by purpose. I had absolutely no backup plan and no customers or even contacts. I look back now at my naivety. I was just absolutely sure I could make it work. I knew I could help others improve their sales."

Like many people setting up on their own, the biggest shock for Dylis was leaving a team of colleagues. Suddenly there was no IT department or marketing department to contact to sort out the problems. Many people never network beyond their own company offices, and the same was true for Dylis.

"In spite of not having a single contact outside the company, it never occurred to me to get another job. I just knew I was going to set up on my own. What doesn't kill you," laughs Dylis, "makes you stronger."

The beginning

Dylis started her working life as a bank cashier at the age of 16. She left and had children, then returned to the bank part-time. A customer of the bank invited staff to visit his warehouse to buy clothes at cost price. Dylis went there every Sunday morning and when friends started complimenting her on her clothes, she decided to start her own clothing business. She borrowed £500, bought some stock and launched Dyl's Togs.

Meanwhile she learnt typing at a night class and after passing her exams, started typing theses for students. Soon she was asked to teach typing at the night class herself. She had no qualifications as a teacher, but they thought she could do it.

"I thought I'd give it a try and see what happened. It would either flop or be good – I could move on from there. I learnt shorthand one week and then started teaching it the next." She worked two days in the bank while her mum looked after the children. In the evenings her husband looked after the children while she taught shorthand and typing, typed theses for students and sold clothes.

"This is how it was. I never had a career plan. Doors have opened and I've said, 'I'll give it a go.' If you are not frightened to step out of your comfort zone, you will have the best chance to succeed. And it was at this point that I had another opportunity come my way.

"The financial services arm of the bank asked me to consider becoming a financial adviser. I went for an interview and was offered a job. I decided I could always go back to selling clothes. But once I took on the work I loved it. The job involved ringing 500 names, at a rate of 60 per week, from the phone directory. I would be cold-calling people in the evening from a little desk in my house. My first night I made eight appointments.

"For me I wasn't selling insurance, I was selling clients a financial safety net – so they could maintain a similar standard of living in the event of their income stopping for whatever reason. I was very passionate about it because I'd experienced financial hardship in my own life as a teenager. I was keen for others to avoid the same trauma. I went on to be the highest life assurance seller in the region.

"After 12 months in the job as financial adviser we moved to Oxford and within six months I was promoted to field sales manager. It was full-time but I worked around the children. I did everything with the girls – homework, Girl Guides, ice-skating, horse-riding, jewellery, quilting.

"As field sales manager I recruited my own team. I showed them how to do the job and be successful at it. We were passionate, charismatic and genuinely a very successful team. If I wanted excellence, I had to show them what excellence looked like. People don't get up in the morning to do a bad job. You need to show them how to do it right. Eight years later I was promoted to regional director. I was in charge of 70 advisers and seven field sales managers at the age of 39. I loved it. We were always in the top five percent for everything. Then, after seven years, the boss turned really nasty."

How to find your first customer

Dylis had walked out on her job and set up on her own. But there she was, facing a blank piece of paper and with a mortgage to pay. How do you find your first customer?

"I wrote it down. My goal was to earn X amount of money. I had earned a lot of money in my last job so I worked out what

I needed. From that I knew I needed to work with people who could pay and would pay. I went straight into the blue-chip market. My marketing plan included a list of companies that I wanted to contact. There was no social networking back then so I reached for the Yellow Pages. I made calls to receptionists and PAs and introduced myself. I got their names and the names of the decision-makers in their organisation. I repeat, I had no names to contact when I left my job. I needed to get the gate-keepers on my side and find out about them and the sales direc-tors. After my initial conversation with the PAs, I told them that I would be in touch and then I'd phone a week later and say, 'Hi Alison, it's Dylis just ringing to talk to Peter.'

"And it worked. That is how I got my first customer. I explained that I was training sales managers, shared the results I had achieved in the past and suggested that we meet. In that first meeting I used everything to establish my credibility and showed them why they could trust me, why they should listen to me and how I could benefit them. My first work was three 40-minute sessions at a convention of top performers in Brighton. I didn't know what to charge so I charged my daily rate and when they said yes I couldn't believe it – I nearly choked."

But having got her first job Dylis then needed to deliver. "I recall driving down to the Grand Hotel in Brighton and being scared to death. I had prepared my 40-minute sessions and practised, practised and practised. I delivered the three sessions and received brilliant feedback.

"After that experience I had grown as a person, my confidence had returned. My comfort zone had become a lot bigger. I firmly believe that you can do anything if you want it enough and you prepare and practise. This was the beginning of my path to my own successful business."

A tadpole in the ocean

"Now I had established a customer base and received recommendations, I got various projects with other banks. But I was a tadpole in the ocean. There was a lot of competition from big training companies. I had to get across why I was better than they were. I wasn't cheap, but I wasn't as expensive as they were. Often the competitors' training would be delivered by an individual who wasn't as experienced as I was. I gathered up some great testimonials to support my credentials. People follow what others do. Third-party references prompt other people to want what you have to offer. In addition, I keep reading, reading, reading and learning – upskilling myself all the time.

"I believe if you want something enough you will get it. Find a way to be the best that you can be. I'm proud that I'm still running my own business after twelve years and adding value to other people's businesses and making a difference to their results." And she has diversified to fit in with changes in her lifestyle, so she now runs workshops. "I'm getting older and I can't be travelling extensively forever. There's also a ceiling if there's just you."

So she set up the latest part of her business, Increase Your Sales in 30 Days. "By expanding on products, seminars, training packages, it's a way of multiplying yourself."

Dylis's Secrets
TO DREAM BUSINESS SUCCESS

1 Get your goals and plans written down. A study by Harvard University stated that the three percent of business people who had their goals written down earned more collectively than the other 97 percent put together.

2 Your marketing strategy should include both online and offline: direct mail, speaking engagements, phone calls, emails, social media, etc.

3 Work out where you are strong and where you are not so strong. Are you good at finding prospective clients and making appointments but not so good at converting appointments into sales? All of these activities can be learnt.

4 My big principle: give to receive. Give something away of value in exchange for an email address. Develop a relationship with the people on that list. Grow your platform with articles, blogs, tweets and point back to what you're giving away for free. Keep building your customer base. Two percent of people buy on their first contact. Eighty percent of business is being made between the fifth contact and the twelfth.

Continued overleaf

"

5 Hire the best people affordable. In hindsight I should have hired more people to help earlier on, rather than do everything myself. At the time I was convinced only I could do it. But now I work with fantastic freelancers at Elance and Fiverr.

6 Expose yourself, so to speak, so you're everywhere. Start to position yourself as the expert and clients will seek you out.

7 Your mindset is very important. You will need to be prepared to overcome challenges. Your mind moves to the most dominant thought and your actions follow. You can only change your actions by changing your thought process first. People sometimes blame head office or personnel or whine that 'I'd be brilliant if…' Change your thought processes and *be* brilliant, don't make excuses. When faced with problems and challenges, don't put your energy into worrying. Channel that energy into finding a solution. Look at your options and find a way to be the best you can be.

8 Always think about what's in it for your customer. Nobody really wants to pay for your product or service. What they want to pay for is something that will enhance their lives, help achieve their objectives or prevent pain.

"

Dylis's attitude to the recession

For Dylis, the recession has actually created more opportunities. "We are bombarded with negativity by the press but there are still businesses out there making money. Don't let the negativity of a recession engulf you. You just have to be the provider of choice. It's important to keep your marketing machine going. Marketing should be a daily activity and sales skills should be sharpened on a regular basis. Otherwise you will suffer the feast and famine of sales and income. Much of your marketing should be on auto-pilot and working even when you're asleep. Apple, Facebook, Microsoft and many more, they all started in a recession and they've all become hugely successful.

"Redundancies are forcing more people to set up as entrepreneurs. Those people will need web designers, accountants, coaching and sales training. The opportunities are still out there with new and existing businesses. Let them know you are there, don't be the 'The World's Best Kept Secret.'"

COACHING TIPS #11
Sell, sell, sell! Everyone can be a successful sales person

If there's one thing that is guaranteed to bring about goosebumps and gasps of horror, it is the idea of selling. It conjures up foot-in-the-door double-glazing salesmen and pavement chuggers, and there's an indefinable whiff of seediness, neediness and all-round toe-curling discomfort around selling.

But sell you must – constantly and relentlessly. Now before you close the book and think this business lark is not for me, think again. There are countless ways to sell that can feel comfortable, helpful and effortless.

Reframe the idea of selling. Think instead of setting out your services as being helpful. Yes, really, *helpful*.

For example, if you were looking for a special wedding outfit or new suit and you entered an upmarket boutique, would you expect the sales assistant to show you just a skirt or just the trousers of a suit? Would it be helpful of the shop assistant – because they didn't want to come over as pushy – to not reveal to you the jacket, hat, bag, cuff-links, ties, shirts, stoles, jewellery, shoes or underwear that would be the perfect accompaniment to said garment?

Selling can be seen as showing a client how you can help them. It's up to them if they want to trawl the shops for evermore seeking a co-ordinating skirt or set of trousers to the wedding jacket – but first why not show them what you have to offer and help them see why shopping with you benefits them?

If your marketing is working well, then orders, clients and customers come forth willingly and easily. But there will be lots of times when you will actively have to sell to a new customer and you will need to feel comfortable with this unless you wish to lose business.

Testimonials and leveraging who you know

If you have happy clients, ask them for testimonials. This is a great way of showing potential new business that you have success stories that they can relate to, e.g. "Brenda lost six stone with me," "Brian got the job with our help," "Using X utterly changed my life – Terry of Tunbridge Wells, Jerry of Brisbane," etc.

Some people have photos of their happy clients, too, and why not consider filming your fans to add authenticity? So be sure to ask for feedback. It's vital.

Point potential customers to these testimonials to show them how you work and your success rate. It provides credibility and reassurance to the newbie shopper.

And why not offer referral fees to your best customers too? If they pass your name on and that lead becomes a client, reward them with a bunch of flowers or discount, and never underestimate the power of a £20 M&S thank you voucher in the post to show goodwill.

Let your raving fans be your best sales team.

The psychology of selling

When it comes to selling, the first thing you must leave at the door is yourself. Yes, you are passionate about your business, you are passionate that you can help people, that your gadget or service is the best, but when it comes to selling it's not about you.

Listen very closely to what your customer really wants – then connect with it. Relay it back to them – "So your time-management issues are really impacting your life right now?" or "I understand you'd like to have more financial peace of mind? What would change if we could help you with that?"

Keep asking potential customers questions and empathise and reassure. It's their needs and their requirements they seek to address so don't bludgeon them with your boastful claims. Be relatable.

Toolbox tips

- Think – what do they need to hear from you? What will convince them?

- What emotions do you need to ignite in them – excitement, inspiration, reassurance?

- What guarantees can you offer? How can you 'blow the doors off'?

- How can you portray your understanding of the client's needs, be onside with them, make them feel special, understood?

- What are you doing to allay their fears and put their minds at ease?

- Soothe not prove – be the balm they want.

- Detach yourself from how you feel about your product; don't take their hesitation personally.

- Know when to step back and let the customer come to you.

Overcoming objections

When it comes to people rejecting your offer, the common misconception is that it is because of the price. This is rarely the case. People buy with their hearts, when they can relate to the product, when they feel confident it is right for them. Buyers want to feel they are taking minimal risk.

If you get people saying it isn't exactly what they were looking for – then ask what would be? Could you customise something to suit their needs? Offer a staggered pricing plan or add value with extras, e.g. maintenance support, loyalty discounts, membership benefits, money back unless satisfied – these can also be ways to secure a sale.

You must be sure your service or product delivers one of the following benefits and be sure your potential sale is aware of this: improves, saves time and money, grows, accelerates, maximises potential, strengthens, adds, reduces the negative, enhances, satisfies, liberates.

How much?

When a potential customer does say that what you are offering is beyond their budget, don't just leave it at that.

Keep asking questions to find out the real reason they aren't buying. Explain how working with you could be an investment for them and enquire politely, "How much is too expensive?"

Get onside with the client's objection by acknowledging their point. "It may seem expensive and I can understand that it seems a lot of money to you but other clients in your situation have said…"

Gently reassure by flagging up the benefits to them, your guarantees and how they may save money and time in the long run by using your services.

When closing the deal, Dylis Guyan recommends agreeing a way forward with a comment like, "So if we can make that sort of savings for you, would you be happy to proceed on the basis of our initial discussion?"

Offer to follow up in a few days if the customer is still undecided. This gives you a chance to assess the client's situation, research and come back with an even more persuasive offer. "I've been thinking a lot about your situation, Suzy, and..."

Who's calling? Maximising a sales call

When a potential customer calls, be sure to have a sales process already in place so that you make the most of the enquiry. Here is a simple guideline but you should create one that suits your brand and style:

Answer the phone in an upbeat way, with a smile in your voice, and say the company name clearly.

Establish why they are calling, what they are looking for specifically; let them do most of the talking.

What might you be picking up between the lines that you can relay back to them? "Sounds like you're raring to go / You must be very tired of looking / You sound great – just the sort of people we work with!"

What do they need to hear from you? Yes, that you can help them – but what else?

Explain how you work without being pushy; sound positive and excited and keen to work with them.

Then they ask, "So how much will this cost?" – don't give the figure straightaway.

Keeping in mind everything you have gleaned about the caller, feed this back to them but also add in all the benefits, add-ons, success rates and follow-up service.

So, say what you can do, the solution (their specific one), and the reassurance they want to hear and then say the price.

If it's appropriate, ask them what your competitors have quoted, which then gives you the opportunity to explain how you differ, your USP and why using your company will be right for them.

If they do not commit there and then, offer to phone them back in a few days.

Finally, don't forget to ask how they heard about you. It's important to track how your marketing is working for you.

CHAPTER 12

Shift happens

66 In the UK half of us dream about starting a business but only 5.8 percent actually set one up. 99

Michael Hayman
Financial Times, 31 August 2012

"I've gone very far on quite a little talent."

Shed (Sheridan) Simove

S HED SIMOVE INVENTS novelty products. I wanted to include him because of his playful approach to work and life. He's also the author of *Success Or Your Money Back* so he's thought about the meaning and the secrets of 'success.' The first secret, he says, is that "anyone (and that means you and I, too) can make it big."

DREAM BUSINESS OWNER

Shed Simove
Novelty gifts – often rude, always amusing,
UK

JOURNEY

TV producer ➡ Creator of a million novelty gifts

A job with Disney at 21 made him see that capitalism and entertainment could be connected. He worked in television for 15 years before deciding to leave. He fully believes we live in an age of opportunity. "Technology allows us to do so much ourselves. With the internet, knowledge is no longer power. The competitive edge is now in creativity. The internet enables you to access resources, so you can become an expert within minutes, and to reach an audience in a few hours. The potential is very exciting.

225

"I've never had a career and the idea of a career turns me cold. I want to live my life in an exciting, interesting, fun way, to make every day one that stimulates me greatly. If that also allows me to shop at Waitrose – brilliant. If it doesn't I'll shop at Sainsbury's, but I'll still be happy."

Starting out

"I saw some novelties in a shop one day and I thought, 'I wonder if I could do that.' I looked into it and went round lots of companies but they all rejected me. So I got on the net and through Alibaba.com I found a manufacturer in China. I made lots of mistakes but got some products out. It's too easy to say the rest is history – it's hard work, but it's empowering. These days you can find someone to help you really quickly."

A believer in the creativity of the brain and enjoying life to the fullest, Shed also understands the fear that holds people back.

"I always look at the worst-case scenario. As a neurotic, I go through carefully what could actually go wrong, and when you deconstruct that, as long as no one dies or is mentally scarred, then pretty much anything else is surmountable. As long as you don't risk your house. And sometimes you *could* risk your house. If you look at the worst-case scenario, that often frees you up because it prepares you.

"When we're growing up we're very much imbued with this idea of pass or fail and I think that's wrong. In my life, like a scientist I have a hypothesis, or a goal – it's something I think will happen, or hope will happen. I *make* it happen and then I have a result. All that matters when you're doing an experiment is that you carry it out and get some results, because those results can inform your next experiment and bring you closer to success or move you in a different direction."

Shed understands the attraction of a guaranteed salary – which he no longer has. Even so, while he has no regrets, he does wish he'd started out on his entrepreneurial journey sooner.

Dip your toe in the water

"Not having financial security does bother me, and it's a real, practical problem. But you don't have to leave your job and start from nothing. You can dip your toe in the water to try out a new target, a new adventure, a new career, without leaving your old one. You have to be really disciplined about it and you might have to get up an hour earlier; you might have to do it in your lunch time; you might have to do it sneakily at work. It's hard but it's possible. There are lots of ways now with the internet to explore and to actually physically start making other things happen while holding on to your day job.

"I find human convention very odd, that people can work 9–5 five days a week and have only two days off – why can't our whole life be off? Or our whole life be *on*, in a way we'd like it to be on. I feel like I'm the little boy shouting at the emperor, saying he's not wearing any clothes."

Novelty Shed

Shed is a novelty in himself. Fairly diminutive with a winning manner, he wheels around a suitcase full of funny, economically produced joke gifts. One of my favourites has recently been banned. Shed's Fifty Shades of Grey notebook – the paper gets increasingly darker – faced an injunction from the publishers of the novel by E.L. James. And sometimes things like that happen. But it doesn't put Shed off. "There's always a way," he says – upbeat, ever hopeful and optimistic.

No one can stop you

"It's a different time now. No one can stop you from posting on the internet and reaching billions of people. That's the most significant thing in our lifetime. It allows anyone to have a chance to reach others. There are lots of souls that are screaming in offices and they have massive talent but that talent's not being utilised – it's criminal. But the printing press is no longer controlled by rich magnates. We've all got a printing press now.

"The only way that humanity has any hope is through understanding intelligence and creativity, because creativity provides solutions for our problems. It also enables you to see the other side of someone's argument, which is a useful tool to have if you're a human."

Life is one big experiment for Shed. He revels in just how much you can do by trial and error. But finding experts has been key in helping him produce his bestselling products.

"One of the ways I've got help is by going to trade fairs. There you will find lots of experts in the new area that you're trying to break into, all in one venue. And because they're in selling mode, I don't pitch to them there and then, I simply get their business cards. As I walk around, I see which stands are well presented, who has good ideas, who's nice, who interacts well with others. Then, weeks later, when they're less busy, I write to them and ask would they ever work with a third party who has ideas. And if they say yes, I go in and meet them. Then I pitch to them. And then, if I'm successful, I work with them."

Transition

"I really wish someone had pestered me at school and found that I had a latent ability to think differently. Although I think we can all do that, I had it naturally. I wish someone had told me in the early days you could be an entrepreneur and work for yourself. I might have had a quicker start. But never mind, I've had good times and I've learnt lots.

"What occurred to me was, if you were a creative person and you wanted to see your ideas come to life, in television there are just so many barriers and so many factors affecting whether a show gets made. The quality of the idea for a TV show is not linked to whether it actually gets on air, which is laughable, but true. This was highly frustrating for me as a creative. Was I going to go around the world pitching monkey tennis or was I going to go into a different area?"

Business novice

"I'd never run a business before and I haven't been to business school. No one ever told me what a balance sheet was. Without being flippant, if you've got more money coming in than you have going out you make a profit. You can buy shoes and take a girl out for a date. It's not brain surgery. Sometimes I don't even look at the figures – I'm not a great businessman and many creative people aren't. I'm sensible. I'll set a cap on how much I'll pay out for a limited run on my new product or I look at my finances and think I can afford to lose that amount – anything over that it would lead me to have problems. It's all very calculated and it pretty much always works out."

Finding a way

"I'm totally winging it. And I think most adults are winging it. I haven't got amazing knowledge or a million followers on Twitter. I'm not a marketing genius. What I am, perhaps, is a genius at thinking up products that capture people's imagination.

"But, actually that's not enough. You need genius PR too. The genius of a PR company is two-fold. Number one, they create a story around the product. Number two, they get it into the hands of the right people – and that's really hard.

"I go to an expert when I haven't got the skills to do what's necessary (which is pretty much all the time). I'm good at ideas but I'm not good at shipping. So I go to a third party. They deal with Debenhams – I don't have to worry about a shipment not coming in – OK, I make less money, but it plays to my strengths and it means I can do more things."

Shed hired a PR company to promote his book, *What Every Man Thinks About Apart From Sex*. It resulted in some TV and newspaper coverage. It got him to No. 44 in the Amazon charts. It consists of 200 blank pages. Yes, blank pages.

"A hard-nosed businessman would take a different line about spending money on a PR company, but for me there's a bigger picture. It sent me on adventures. Publishers from other countries contacted me. I had more adventures attending the book launch. So even if it didn't make me a fortune, I have a brilliant story and my life's richer.

"Because I wing it all the time, I make a million mistakes every single day. You never know if something's going to take off. That's what's interesting and frustrating. I like to think that everything I bring out is genius and everything is going to rock the world. Of course, it doesn't! Still, as it turned out, *What Every Man Thinks* did make me some money. I don't believe in luck. I made a great product. I designed it really carefully. I hired a great PR company that seeded it well and I had fantastic images of it and a very simple video. All those factors gave it the biggest chance of success.

"For me it's about looking back at little lifebuoys on the sea of my life, and, even if other people don't think they're that amazing, the fact I released a blank book – in my dark times, it makes me chuckle."

Shed's biggest challenge

"A constant challenge is keeping an eye on standards. If you're doing something yourself and you care about it, you're thrilled by it, driven by it. You want it to be as good as you can with the time and money you have. Sometimes it's a challenge when not everyone's got the same vision as you.

"I worked in TV and I felt like I knew what I was doing at the end and I was good at it. But now in all my entrepreneurial activities I'm literally chucking mud at the wall every day. I'm just doing the best I can. I'm simply thinking, 'Would I like this if someone sold it, or gave it, to me?'"

Shed's biggest success

"Doing stuff I want to do in the day. Eating delicious food and going to great places. Being fulfilled in a large way by what I do. Having a fun, interesting, varied life and meeting amazing people. If you look at my bank account, I lurch from boom to bust, but I'd rather be successful in life.

"Even though I know I'm not curing cancer when I'm making a novelty notepad, it gives me pleasure that people will like it. I also like going to companies and talking about innovation and creativity and the techniques I use for those. Because you feel like you are engaging with another human and perhaps helping them in a way that other humans helped me when I was young. The biggest trick is not having your soul screaming, as it sometimes did when I was working in a company."

Shed's Secrets

TO DREAM BUSINESS SUCCESS

66

1 Focus on what excites you and focus on what would give you a thrill if it happened and then move towards that.

2 Work with the best people you can, people who also care and who know what they're doing and have done it before and made mistakes.

3 Write your idea down. Find someone who can help you bring the idea to life in a very small way, through visualisation or a prototype.

4 Reliability is absolutely pivotal in business and the crux on which everything lies.

5 Avoid 'negnets' – negative magnets – the people who hear your ideas and say, 'That's not very good.' The crime isn't having a rubbish idea – your brain will let you know that soon enough. The crime is the negativity that stops you from doing something new. If you don't do anything new you'll stagnate. So don't be too cautious. Yes, be sensible, minimise your risks. But mistakes are part of the process, they are a sign that you are (hallelujah!) doing something.

6 The most important thing is just to start, really. Most people don't even start.

99

COACHING TIPS #12
Summary

Over the past ten years of having my own business I have had the privilege of coming across hundreds of entrepreneurs of all shapes, sizes, ages and flavours. From a retired woman who 'waits at home' on behalf of busy executives to let in workmen, handle deliveries and walk dogs to international CEOs whose franchise ideas have gone global.

What I have learned is that you don't have to possess superhuman powers of steely nerve, business mastery or elite expertise. What unites these people who literally 'make' their own money is a certain positivity, a passion and, in an uncannily large number of cases, a slightly wild look in their eyes.

Their five-mile stare is the trademark of the entrepreneur in repose, concentrating on their big dream, on their clients, and their creativity constantly ticking away to see how they can grow and develop their enterprise. You can be like them. It is in you. You have what it takes.

You don't have to be extraordinary – you just have to want it enough and truly believe you can do it and be prepared to put in the work. Generating your own sales is a deeply satisfying experience. It validates you and your idea both financially and emotionally and there is nothing more rewarding than seeing your bank account fill up from the results of your ideas and labours.

Looking back, being made redundant was the best career move ever made for me. I could sweat blood thinking of what my life would have been like if I had stayed on at a newspaper that was rapidly declining, with no promise of meaningful work beyond it.

I see past colleagues still suffering the fallout and scrapping around doing badly paid freelance work to make ends meet. There is no such thing as a job for life now and it's the wise guy or gal who considers building an entrepreneurial escape tunnel before leaving the day job.

You already possess specialist knowledge, know-how or skills that others will pay for if you provide a solution for them. That's called being an entrepreneur.

So if you are drowning in the mediocrity of being a wage slave and plagued by the sinking feeling on the rainy Monday commute that there's got to be more to life than this, start looking above the parapet.

Join courses, research, listen to talks and read biographies on how other people have done it. Dare to be curious and in the spirit of curiosity stick your nose in and look around. What have you got to lose except your current dissatisfaction?

The easiest first step to take is to list what you don't want. Part of our human condition is to want to move away from painful or uncomfortable things so the What I Don't Want list writes itself.

The challenge is to step toward the positive, toward the things that make our hearts sing, that brighten our eyes. It may be a journey of discovery to ask yourself, "What does excite me?" So take time to explore new possibilities for joy and fulfilment. For many this may even be for the first time.

Look to your heroes – what is it about them, their achievements, the qualities they possess that might be a signpost to what inspires you or resonates with you?

Change does not have to be terrifying; it can be thrilling, and when the dust settles after losing a job you could find that the best opportunity ever lies before you.

Recently a coach I know sheepishly said that she was returning to paid work because "I miss colleagues / fancy a change / it will only be for a few months." The more reasons she gave the more apologetic she sounded. I worked out she was embarrassed to go back to a Jay-Oh-Be (job).

Trust me, you'll never be embarrassed to say that you're starting your own business.

Good luck. May you never look back.

Carole Ann Rice

AFTERWORD

This book is a 'business' and I have tried to apply to it all the advice you find in it.

Like the businesses showcased here, the book started from nothing. It was a seed of an idea in my mind, and it grew painfully slowly at times. Luckily, my interviewees unwittingly kept me going! Their emphasis on the importance of mindset and attitude, perseverance and dealing with problems spurred me on. I also felt glad to have the partnership of my co-writer Carole Ann, who understood the difficulties, and met up with me to revitalise and inspire the process. The 'dynamic double act,' in which Rosie and Sophie delight in having someone to share it all with, immediately resonated with me.

I have taken on board the message in the book that you can't do it all and I have sought advice from experts along the way. In addition, I have braced myself and networked as the book advises, and met some amazing people.

How will Carole Ann and I measure the success of our business? A healthy financial return would be nice, and we look forward to 'improving sales in 30 days,' as prescribed by Dylis Guyan. But like the other businesses appearing here, it's not about the money. A bigger reward would be to hear that the book has not only been an inspiration but has been of use in the first steps to setting up your dream business.

Sarah Wade

FURTHER READING

Rachel Bridge, *How to Make a Million Before Lunch* (Virgin Books, 2011)

Rachel Bridge, *How to Start a Business Without Any Money* (Virgin Books, 2012)

Antonia Chitty, *The Mumpreneur Guide: Start Your Own Successful Business* (Book Shaker, 2011)

Antonia Chitty & Erica Douglas, *Blogging: The Essential Guide* (Need2Know, 2012)

Antonia Chitty & Erica Douglas, *Making Money Online* (Robert Hale Ltd, 2012)

Sophie Cornish & Holly Tucker, *Build a Business From Your Kitchen Table* (Simon and Schuster, 2012)

Suzy Greaves, *Making the Big Leap: Coach Yourself to Create the Life You Really Want* (New Holland, 2004)

Emma Jones, *Turn Your Talent into a Business: A Guide to Earning a Living From Your Hobby* (Harrison House, 2011)

Ken Robinson & Lou Aronica, *The Element: How Finding Your Passion Changes Everything* (Penguin Books, 2009)

Peter Sims, *Little Bets: How Breakthrough Ideas Emerge from Small Discoveries* (Random House, 2012)

Sarah Wade & Carole Ann Rice, *Find Your Dream Job* (Marshall Cavendish, 2009)

ABOUT THE AUTHORS

Sarah Wade

Carole Ann Rice

SARAH WADE lives in West London with a Shakespeare-obsessed academic and a Lego-obsessed small son. Her own obsessions include interviewing people who like their jobs. She likes her own – a producer for BBC radio – but also likes writing books, such as *Find Your Dream Job* (Marshall Cavendish, 2009), and her blog, www.findyourdreamjob. wordpress.com.

66 It's been a privilege to meet the business owners in this book. All have survived a recession and they are driven by an infectious passion for their work. Their advice has enabled me to deal with the challenges of trying to get a product to market. As it reaches the bookshelves I intend to continue to apply their business tips because their advice is like gold dust.

I'd like to thank all the contributors and everyone who helped me find them, as well as everyone I have spoken to in the process, Neil, Justin Lau, Martin Liu, Andy Milligan, John Simmons, COCC, Umang Panchal, Shed Simove, Alex Butler Kindred HQ, Moy McGowan, Kath, Jenny & Darren @ hotsquash.com, and Ross Coker.

Finally, I dedicate this book to Neil, Dixie and my Dad. 99

CAROLE ANN RICE has been managing director of her own coaching practice, The Real Coaching Company, for the past ten years, with diverse clients ranging from the London School of Economics and Visa through to scientists and rock stars.

An award-winning journalist and one-time TV presenter, Carole Ann Rice is the only life coach in the UK to have her own column in a national daily newspaper – 'Happy Mondays', which appears weekly in the *Daily Express*. She has also written for *The Sun*, *The Mirror* and the *Independent on Sunday*, and as a coach has been featured in *The Sunday Times*, *Metro News*, *New Woman*, *Glamour* and *Harper's Bazaar*. In 2013 she co-launched Clever Acorn, an online business training company for start-ups (www.cleveracorn.com).

She is married to a political commentator, has two children and two cats, and lives in West London.

66 There are few things as exciting as making your own money, being your own boss and finding creative solutions for being of service to others. I love the autonomy of being a business owner and the limitless possibilities it presents. It's like having the most absorbing hobby ever – only you get paid to do it. How cool is that?

Acknowledgements: Patrick, Phoebe, Raphael, in memory of Catherine and her gift when it was much needed, Mark, Paullette and all the Fabulous Women – thanks to all for all their love, inspiration and support.

This is for all those who have followed their dream and taken it to market – the ones with the five-mile stare and hope in their hearts. 99